Proofreading

BY
DEBORAH WHITE BROADWATER

ISBN 1-58037-172-8

Printing No. CD-1393

Mark Twain Media, Inc., Publishers
Distributed by Carson-Dellosa Publishing Company, Inc.

Table of Contents

Introduction to the Teacher .... **iv**

Proofreading: Introduction **1**
Proofreading Checklist 2
Proofreading Marks 3

Punctuation—Commas **4**
Introduction 4
Exercise 1 5
Exercise 2 6
Exercise 3 7

Punctuation—End Marks **8**
Introduction 8
Exercise 1 9
Exercise 2 10
Exercise 3 11

Punctuation—Apostrophes/Quotation Marks **12**
Introduction 12
Exercise 1 13
Exercise 2 14

Run-on Sentences/Combining Sentences **15**
Introduction 15
Run-on Sentences: Exercise 1 16
Run-on Sentences: Exercise 2 17
Combining Sentences: Exercise 1 ..18
Combining Sentences: Exercise 2..19

Punctuation Review **20**
Exercise 1 20
Exercise 2 21
Exercise 3 22

Personal Pronouns **23**
Introduction 23
Exercise 1 24
Exercise 2 25

Pronoun Antecedents **26**
Introduction 26
Exercise 1 27
Exercise 2 28

Confusing Verbs **29**
Introduction 29
Exercise 1 30
Exercise 2 31

Subject-Verb Agreement **32**
Introduction 32
Exercise 1 33
Exercise 2 34

Compound Subjects and Indefinite Pronouns **35**
Introduction 35
Exercise 1 36
Exercise 2 37
Exercise 3 38

Subject-Verb Arrangement **39**
Introduction 39
Exercise 1 40

Verb Tense **41**
Introduction 41
Exercise 1 42
Exercise 2 43

Comparisons **44**
Introduction 44
Exercise 1 45
Exercise 2 46

Modifiers/Double Negatives **47**
Introduction 47
Modifiers: Exercise 1 48
Modifiers: Exercise 2 49
Double Negatives: Exercise 1 50
Double Negatives: Exercise 2 51

Table of Contents

Capitalization 52
Introduction 52
Exercise 1 53
Exercise 2 54

Colloquialisms 55
Introduction 55
Exercise 1 56
Exercise 2 57

Proofreading Review 58
Exercise 1 58
Exercise 2 59
Exercise 3 60
Exercise 4 61
Exercise 5 62
Exercise 6 63
Exercise 7 64
Exercise 8 65
Exercise 9 66
Exercise 10 67
Exercise 11 68
Exercise 12 69
Exercise 13 70
Exercise 14 71
Exercise 15 72
Exercise 16 73
Exercise 17 74
Exercise 18 75
Exercise 19 76
Exercise 20 77

Answer Keys 78

Introduction to the Teacher

Errors in writing destroy the message. In today's world, it is important to be able to communicate well. Students study the writing process from rough draft to final published product. One very important step is proofreading. No matter how well a paper is written, it will not be well accepted unless spelling, punctuation, grammar, and usage are well done.

This book is intended to offer the teacher and the parent lessons to help the student practice proofreading. In this book, there are explanations of what to look for when proofreading. These pages may be copied, and the student can keep them in a three-ring binder to use as a resource when they are proofreading their papers or others' papers. Each proofreading skill has a page or two of sentences to practice the skill, followed by a paragraph to proofread for the specific skill. At the end of the book, there are also paragraphs and stories that are written with errors so students can go through and make corrections. This will give students the opportunity to practice their proofreading skills before proofreading their peers' papers.

Teachers may use these activities when teaching proofreading to the whole class as a part of the writing workshop. They may also use the activities for students having specific problems with proofreading. Some students may understand after one activity, while others may need additional practice. The paragraphs and longer stories may be used as applications of the whole proofreading experience.

Proofreading: *Introduction*

Proofreading means to actually read proofs. A proof is the copy of the book or story that a printer would make in order to check to see if the type had been set correctly. This was done because mistakes were almost always made when the type was set, and this gave the printer an opportunity to correct these mistakes. The people who checked the proofs were called proofreaders.

When you write your story, play, or book, you will also make mistakes. You or a classmate will be your proofreader. There are many areas your teacher will want you to check before you turn in your work. You will have to check for grammar and make sure you have used the correct verb tense, pronouns, subject-verb agreement, and modifiers. You will also need to look at the spelling in your writing. Capitalization and punctuation are two other areas that will be checked as you proofread.

It is always difficult to proofread your own paper. As you read it, you read what you thought you wrote and not what you actually wrote. A classmate will probably do a better job of proofreading your work than you will. Find someone who you feel is a careful reader, and ask him or her if they would proofread your paper. Don't feel that they will be judging you or your paper. Think of them as a proofreader you have employed to help you do the best with your writing assignment.

If you cannot find someone to proofread your paper for you, there are a couple of things you can do to help you be your own proofreader. Put your paper aside for a day or two before you go over it. This will help you think more about what you are reading instead of what you think you wrote. Another trick is to start at the end of your paper and read it backwards. When you proofread this way, you are looking at each of the words and will more easily see if any are misspelled. You can also take color markers or pens and go through your paper and underline the subject in one color and underline the verb in another color; then draw an arrow from the subject to the verb. This will help you check if your subjects and verbs agree or if you have sentence fragments or run-on sentences.

Proofreading takes a lot of thinking. You cannot just quickly read through the writing and then pronounce that the piece is finished. In order to be a good writer, it is important to be a good proofreader too. You need to be able to communicate with others, and if your writing has errors, you will not be able to communicate well.

Proofreading Checklist

Here is a checklist of things to think about and look for as you proofread your own paper or someone else's paper.

1. Check that each word is spelled correctly. If you have any questions, use a dictionary or a spell checker.
2. Check each sentence to see that it has correct end punctuation. Should the mark be a period, a question mark, or an exclamation point?
3. Check to see that each sentence begins with a capital letter and that all proper nouns and adjectives are capitalized.
4. Check to see that each sentence has a subject and a verb. Make sure the subject and the verb agree in number and in tense. Make sure that the same tense is used throughout the paper.
5. Check to see that the correct pronouns are used and that they agree with the antecedents.
6. Check for confused verbs; make sure that they are used correctly.
7. Check to see that apostrophes are used correctly for contractions and possession.
8. Check that double negatives are not used.
9. Check to see that the correct modifier is used. Is it a comparison or a superlative?
10. Check to make sure that colloquialisms are not used. Most papers require formal English.
11. Check to see if there are run-on sentences, and then correct the punctuation.
12. Check for sentence fragments. Does the sentence need a subject or a verb?

Proofreading Marks

There are special marks that are used in proofreading. These marks are called proofreading marks. Sometimes there are slight variations in the marks. As you go through your paper or someone else's, you should use the marks to show where errors have occurred.

Proofreaders often use red pens or pencils to make proofreading marks, so the marks are more visible. For the exercises in this book, your teacher will tell you if you should use a red pen or pencil.

Spelling	Ofen I misspell words.
Capitalize	bill wrote the note.
Lower case	I know my Dad is home.
Add a period	We played basketball
Add a word, letter, or punctuation	Where is the book?
Add a blank space	Send Keri topick up the papers.
Add a comma	Mike our captain called the plays.
Add an apostrophe	Dont you think it is cold?
Add quotation marks	Do we need coats? Jeff asked.
Take out a letter, word, or phrase	Do you you want a sandwich?
Reverse words or letters	The bike belonged to me and my sister.
Indent	On the first day of camp, I broke my arm.
New paragraph	... we put out the campfire. The next morning ...

Punctuation—Commas: *Introduction*

Commas are used between words and to show a pause. Commas are also used in a series of words or ideas to keep them from running together. The comma is one of the most important punctuation marks, but it is also the most overused.

Use a comma **to separate items in a series of three or more.**

Example: We had sandwiches, potato salad, and cupcakes in our picnic lunch.

Use a comma **to separate the digits in a number.**

Example: The population of the United States is over 250,000,000.

Use a comma **to separate the city and state or country in an address and the day, month, and year in a date.**

Examples: London, England, is her address. He is from Phoenix, Arizona.
The paper is due Friday, September 21, 2001.
January 27, 1801, was a cold day.

Use a comma **to join two simple sentences that are about the same thing into a compound sentence.** Use a connecting word like *and* or *but.*

Examples: I went to the store after school, and I bought two comic books.
Paul likes to build models, but Jose likes to read.

Use a comma **to set off introductory words or phrases from the rest of the sentence.**

Examples: Sorry, I don't know that answer.
In the year 2000, the election results were not finalized for 35 days.

Use a comma **to set off a subordinate clause from an independent clause.**

Examples: When you are finished, please hand in your papers.
Sleet, which is a form of precipitation, occurs mostly in the winter.

Name: ______________________________ Date: ______________

Punctuation—Commas: *Exercise 1*

Directions: Proofread the following sentences carefully. Write correct in the blank below the sentence if it is correct. Rewrite the sentence if it is incorrect, adding commas where needed.

1. "Juan did you do your homework last night?" asked Angela.

   ____

2. I had a banana an orange two carrots and a sandwich for lunch.

   ____

3. "Yes I think it would be a good idea to read the story together" said Mrs. Martinez.

   ____

4. When I went to the ballgame I caught a fly ball.

   ____

5. Laura will write the paper proofread it and then turn it in to the newspaper.

   ____

6. "Ask for a paper, a pencil, and a book," said Mrs. Bloom.

   ____

7. Do you like roses daffodils mums or tulips?

   ____

8. Amy wanted to go to the movies but Beth wanted to play tennis.

   ____

9. Look there is a fox in the backyard.

   ____

10. I have a large dog, and I have a very small cat.

   ____

Name: ______________________________ Date: ____________________

Punctuation—Commas: *Exercise 2*

Directions: Proofread the following paragraph carefully. Using the correct symbol, insert commas where needed.

On January 14 2001 we had the biggest snowstorm in the history of our town. The snow was so deep believe it or not that it came up to my dad's chest. I think the only place that had more snow than our town was Buffalo New York. Snow even though it looks light is very difficult to shovel when it is that deep. It was even too deep for our snow blower but once we had taken off the top layer with a shovel it was easier. My brother sister and I were all outside helping. One of the hardest things to do was to lift the shovel high enough to throw the next shovelful. One time when I wasn't paying attention to what I was doing I threw my shovel of snow and it landed right on my sister who was shoveling on the other side of the snow mound. With that much snow you have to plan where you are going to put the stuff. If you plan it right you can get a really big heap of snow in one spot so later you can build a fort or use the hill to sled down. It is fun to be outdoors with all that snow working with your family but I like it when we are finished and come in for hot chocolate.

Name: ______________________________ Date: ____________________

Punctuation—Commas: *Exercise 3*

Directions: Proofread the following paragraph carefully. Using the correct symbol, insert commas where needed.

"Mrs. Evans will you please help me with question number six?" Caroline asked.

"I think you should ask one of the students in your group," answered Mrs. Evans.

That is how our math class works. We are given assignments each day to work on in math and we work together in groups to solve the problems. Mrs. Evans told us this is the way many important problems are solved in the world.

Sometimes we pick our own groups. When we do I like to be with Becky Ben and Allison. We are all friends. This doesn't always work out because we end up talking about other things and don't always get the problem done. If we were working on a world problem this probably wouldn't be the best group for me to be with.

Other times Mrs. Evans puts us in a group. She will use numbers eye color age or height to decide our groups. We never know what it will be. These groups usually work the best. We don't talk as much about other things and we get more work done. Sometimes there are people who don't work at all but Mrs. Evans said that happens with world problems too.

It would probably be best to look at the class choose the people who work the hardest and work with them. This would help me get my math problems solved. In the world hopefully that is what happens when problems are being solved.

Punctuation—End Marks: *Introduction*

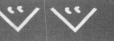

It is important in proofreading to check end marks. These help the reader know where the sentence should end and how it should be read. The three end marks are the period, the question mark, and the exclamation point.

Period

Use at the end of a declarative sentence.	I ate lunch with Jennifer.
Use at the end of an imperative sentence.	Come home right after school.
Use with abbreviations.	Dr. – Doctor Fri. – Friday
Use with an indirect question.	Carol asked Mrs. Evans to repeat the last answer.

Question Mark

Use at the end of an interrogative sentence.	May I borrow your red pen?
	Who is going to the football game?

Exclamation Point

Use at the end of an exclamatory sentence.	Look out for the charging bull!
Use at the end of an interjection.	Ugh!

Name: ______________________________ Date: ______________

Punctuation—End Marks: *Exercise 1*

Directions: Proofread the following sentences carefully. Write correct in the blank below the sentence if it is correct. Rewrite the sentence if it is incorrect, adding periods where needed.

1. My appointment with Dr Jones is Thurs at 4 PM

   ____

2. On Tues I got a letter from St Louis, Missouri, where Mr Anderson lives

   ____

3. The bicycle race will start on Locust St at 10 AM and end at Spruce Ave

   ____

4. Mrs Anderson and Mr Martin are the sponsors of the trip on Mon

   ____

5. J K Rowling writes the Harry Potter books

   ____

6. Jan and Feb are the coldest months of the year.

   ____

7. Ms Walker is going to meet me at 6 PM on Thursday

   ____

8. The ABC Co will be opening its new store on Fri

   ____

9. Dr Wong will be in surgery at the hospital on Maine St

   ____

10. Sen Long lives in Washington, DC, our nation's capital.

    ____

Name: ______________________________________ Date: ____________________

Punctuation—End Marks: *Exercise 2*

Directions: Rewrite the following paragraph on the lines below, using periods in the correct places.

Last week my mom made an appt for me at Dr Warner's office; he is an eye doctor. I had to get my eyes checked. His office is located at 1127 Vermont St My appt was at 1:30 PM I needed to get a pass from Mrs Blanchard, our school secretary She said she thought Dr Warner's office was at 1127 Ohio Ave and not on Vermont St. My mom was right about the address, and I got my eyes checked Now I have another appt with Dr Warner on Thurs, Jan 14, to pick up my glasses. I will tell Mrs Blanchard that Dr Warner's office is on Vermont St and not on Ohio Ave

____

____

____

____

____

____

____

____

____

____

____

____

____

____

Name: ______________________________ Date: ____________________

Punctuation—End Marks: *Exercise 3*

Directions: Proofread the following sentences carefully. Use the insert mark to insert the correct word, punctuation, exclamation point, or question mark.

1. I think the ball off the table and onto the floor.
2. Where would you like to go on vacation this summer
3. Wow look at the beautiful sunset tonight.
4. If you could have three wishes would they be?
5. Stop car
6. Check the first two or three on the spelling list.
7. Can you draw a map of the original thirteen colonies.

8. Oh. That bursting balloon startled me.
9. What advice would you give a new student to our school about the lunchroom.
10. Mr. Meyer likes to tell to the class to get them to laugh.
11. I think we lost three of the to this jigsaw puzzle.
12. How long have you been waiting in line to buy a ticket.
13. Hey. Why did you throw that water balloon at me?
14. I think Mike's Rover is trying to dig a hole under the fence.
15. It's my turn to wash the dishes and your turn to them.

Punctuation—Apostrophes/Quotation Marks: *Introduction*

Apostrophes are used to show *possession* and to show letters that are left out of words to make *contractions*.

Possession

If the noun is *singular*, add an apostrophe and an "s."

Bill's baseball bat   Jordan's soccer ball

If the noun is *plural and does not end in "s,"* add an apostrophe and an "s."

children's toys   everyone's ticket

If the noun is *plural and does end in "s,"* just add an apostrophe.

boys' umbrellas   skaters' costumes

Contractions

did not	didn't
it is	it's
you will	you'll

Quotation marks are used to enclose the exact words of the speaker.

- The direct quotation is preceded by a comma or a colon.
- The first letter of the direct quotation is capitalized.
- Periods always go inside the quotation marks.

Mary said, "Meet me at the restaurant after work."

- Question marks and exclamation points go inside the quotation marks if they are part of the direct words of the speaker.

Jerry asked, "Are you going to the movies tonight?"

Jenny exclaimed, "I can't believe we won the game!"

Name: ______________________________ Date: ______________

Punctuation—Apostrophes: *Exercise 1*

Directions: Rewrite the following paragraph on the lines below, using apostrophes in the correct places.

Im going to the zoo on Friday with my friends. We will ride in my sisters car. My brother isnt going with us. Hed rather do something with his friend Brock. Well get to see Sarahs father because he works at the zoo. He said that we could see the animals up close because hed take us around the cages. I hope to see my favorite animal. It isnt the lion, and it isnt a giraffe; my favorite animal is the elephant. Well walk to the bird house and watch the birds. Maybe some of the birds feathers will be on the ground and well be able to take one. Going to the zoo is great. I dont know of anywhere thats more fun.

Name: ______________________________ Date: ____________________

Punctuation—Apostrophes/Quotation Marks: *Exercise 2*

Directions: Proofread the following sentences carefully. Use the correct symbol to insert an apostrophe or quotation marks where needed.

1. Ling said, Please open the door and help carry in the groceries.
2. I think its a good book to read and discuss.
3. Carols sweater is in the lost and found in Mrs. Underwoods room.
4. “Mike, asked Dad, did you eat the last piece of cherry pie?”
5. Did you feed the cat its dinner tonight? asked Dad.
6. Panchos going to see if he can meet us at the park tomorrow.
7. Angela, did you get Beths homework?” asked Mom.
8. I think its Barbs or Debbies turn to wash the dishes tonight.
9. Karen cant see the chalkboard without her glasses.
10. “Open your books, but dont begin reading until I tell you to, said Mr. Garcia.
11. Ill need to do my homework early tonight, so I can watch TV.
12. Todd, do you think you’ve eaten enough of the cookies?” Carri complained.
13. Lets see how many free throws we can make in five minutes.
14. “Annie, Mrs. Current called, do you have your mittens, or do you have Mike’s?
15. Look, well bring the cake for the party if you can bring the soda.

Run-on Sentences/Combining Sentences: *Introduction*

Sometimes when you write quickly and are putting your thoughts on paper, run-on sentences occur. **Run-on sentences** are two or more complete sentences that are written as one long sentence without the proper punctuation or conjunction. There are three ways to correct run-on sentences.

- You may make the long sentence into two sentences and use the correct punctuation at the end.
- You may add a comma and a conjunction.
- You may add a semicolon between the two sentences.

Examples:

Run-on:	Draw a large circle divide it in half.
Correct:	Draw a large circle. Divide it in half.
Correct:	Draw a large circle, and divide it in half.
Correct:	Draw a large circle; divide it in half.
Run-on:	I had lunch with my sister then I went outside and I played with my dog.
Correct:	I had lunch with my sister. I went outside. I played with my dog.
Correct:	I had lunch with my sister, and then I went outside. I played with my dog.
Correct:	I had lunch with my sister. I went outside, and I played with my dog.

As you can see, there are many ways to correct run-on sentences. When you make the corrections, you need to be sure that you keep the sentence length interesting to the reader. Too many short, choppy sentences are not interesting.

When you have many short, choppy sentences, it is a good idea to **combine two or more related sentences**. In this way, you can vary the lengths of your sentences.

Sentences may be combined by placing a comma after the first sentence and adding a **coordinating conjunction**, such as *and, or, but,* or *yet,* before the next sentence.

Example: Leave the room. Shut the door.
Leave the room, and shut the door.

You may also combine sentences by making one of the sentences a subordinate clause. The subordinate clause is added to the independent clause with commas and **subordinating conjunctions**, such as *while, because, after,* or *since,* or **relative pronouns**, such as *who, that,* and *which.*

Examples: The train arrived. We reached the station.
The train arrived after we reached the station.

Frank's paper is due tomorrow. It is about slavery.
Frank's paper, which is about slavery, is due tomorrow.

Name: ______________________________ Date: ______________

Run-on Sentences: *Exercise 1*

Directions: Proofread the following sentences carefully. Correct the run-on sentences, using commas, periods, or semicolons.

1. There are eleven girls in our class there are fourteen boys in our class.

   ____

2. Make sure you have your umbrella take your raincoat too.

   ____

3. Jacob is an honor student he always has excellent grades.

   ____

4. William had to stay after school he had been talking during math class.

   ____

5. Benjamin needed to go to soccer practice he couldn't play in the game if he missed.

   ____

6. The railroad built a track through town it brought many new businesses to the area.

   ____

7. Our family is going to the beach for our vacation my brother will have to miss out.

   ____

8. Come over to my house after school I have the information for our project.

   ____

9. I think all I do is write run-on sentences I need to practice my punctuation skills.

   ____

10. When you are giving a speech, it is important to speak in a clear voice don't mumble.

    ____

Name: ______________________________ Date: ____________________

Run-on Sentences: *Exercise 2*

Directions: Use proofreading marks to mark the corrections that need to be made in the following paragraphs.

Have you ever been to the circus? I remember the first time I went with my mom and dad we had a great time. It was two hours long but the time went by in what seemed like just a few minutes.

When we first walked in after buying our tickets we were greeted by clowns. They had on every color in the rainbow and they all had different makeup on their faces. There were happy clowns and there were sad clowns there were even clowns who looked like they had tears running down their faces.

We found our seats, bought some cotton candy and the show began. There were women and men who flew back and forth on the trapeze. It was amazing to watch them let go and then be caught on the other side. There were animal acts with lions and elephants, tigers and dogs, and horses and ponies. Some people walked on a high wire. Didn't slip or fall.

The whole day was wonderful I want to go the next time the circus is in town, it is the best show to watch.

Name: ______________________________ Date: ________________

Combining Sentences: *Exercise 1*

Directions: Proofread the following sentences carefully. Combine the sentences on the lines below.

1. John is on the football team. He is president of our class.

   ____

2. I want to go to the movies. I also need to clean my room.

   ____

3. Jason caught the ball. He almost ran into the fence.

   ____

4. Stephen won the school spelling bee. He couldn't go to the state competition.

   ____

5. Did you ask Lauren to come to the party? Are you going to wait until later to ask her?

   ____

6. Let's have soup for dinner. I will make biscuits.

   ____

7. We're watching videos. Mom is making popcorn.

   ____

8. I could play tennis after school. I could do my homework.

   ____

9. Who brought in the packages? Where did you put my new shirt?

   ____

10. Nick will feed the dog. He won't have time to take her for a walk.

    ____

Name: ____________________ Date: ____________

Combining Sentences: *Exercise 2*

Directions: Rewrite the following paragraph carefully on the lines below, combining sentences as needed.

Last night it snowed. We had to shovel the driveway this morning. It was a difficult job. My older brother Steve helped with it. It took almost all morning. There were three of us shoveling so it went faster. We could have used just shovels. Mr. Adams came with his snow blower.

We came inside. Mom gave us hot chocolate. She put marshmallows in it. We had to hang up our clothes to dry. It didn't take too long. Did we want to go outside again? Did we want to stay in and watch TV?

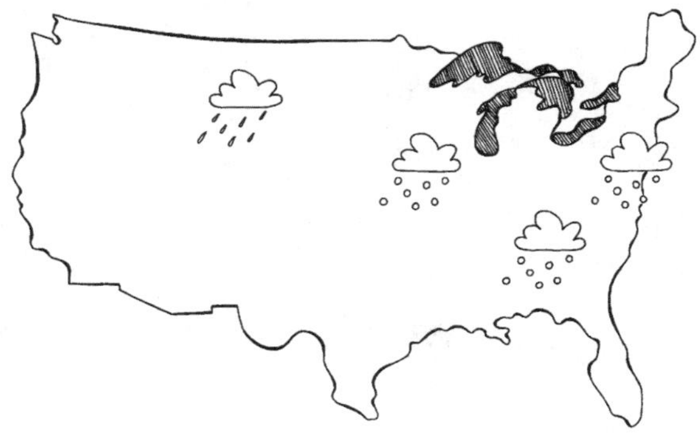

I really like snow days. It's back to school tomorrow. Did I hear the weatherman say there is a chance of snow tomorrow?

Name: ______________________________ Date: ________________

Punctuation Review: *Exercise 1*

Directions: Proofread the following sentences carefully. Use the correct proofreading marks to show where a correction should be made.

1. I wish I didnt need to get a shot at dr. Davis's office.
2. who is that in the red jacket?
3. Isnt that the worst book you have ever read?
4. My dog out the door this morning and jumped over the fence.
5. I never grew plants before. This year I planted petunias?
6. "Yes, Mr. White replied, there are seven layers of rock in the aaquarium."
7. I eat my lunch at 10 40 A.M.
8. Allison Jordan and Taylor are all meating me on thrusday afternoon.
9. I think we need too sheats of paper for the test on monday.
10. Me and Jeff were the only ones brave enough to sled down the hill.
11. Whose got the key to the backdoor?
12. Mr. Meyer the door before class began.
13. Have you ever read *harry potter and the chamber of secrets?*
14. I have live in Le Sueur Minnesota and Waukesha Wisconsin.
15. Which jaars may I use for my Science project?

Name: ____________________________________ Date: __________________

Punctuation Review: *Exercise 2*

Directions: Proofread the following sentences carefully. Use the correct proofreading marks to show where a correction should be made.

1. I am going to see mrs. Ling before schoool tomorrow.
2. do you know how long the appontment will be?
3. Its going to rain tomorrw when we have our picnic.
4. Where idd you find the answer to question number sesven
5. My cat all of the cat food for dinner
6. Are you going too the movies on saturday.
7. I need to rite down your adresss so I can pick you up.
8. If I get the next two two ansers correct I will win the spelling bee.
9. how long do we have too finish the homework assignment?
10. I think I will put the answers on a seperate piece of paper.
11. Carol, Beth, and me are going to decorate the gym ofr the dance.
12. Mrs. Humphrey said, Make sure that all the clay is put away after the art project."
13. This is the forth day of th week.
14. Zack Juan and Sven have no sisters.
15. Do you think me and Miguel will make the baseball team?

Name: ______________________________ Date: ______________

Punctuation Review: *Exercise 3*

Directions: Proofread the following sentences carefully. Use the correct symbol to insert a colon, a comma, or a semicolon.

1. Are you going to the store or are you going to stay home and watch TV?
2. My mom told me to go to the store and buy the following items a head of lettuce, a quart of milk, a loaf of bread and a stick of butter.
3. Who left their coat hat and sweater on the playground?

4. Have you ever been skiing or do you like to stay inside?
5. My brother lives in Oxford Mississippi.
6. After the morning news I go outside and wait for the bus.
7. My best friend is my dog he goes everywhere with me.
8. For school we need these supplies a three-ring binder, loose-leaf paper, a pencil and a red pen.
9. Mr. Evans the custodian helped us decorate the gym for the dance.
10. I have a large orange cat his name is Tigger.
11. Please help me with my homework then we can play on the computer.
12. I would like to have spaghetti salad garlic bread and pudding for dinner tonight.
13. We invited Mrs. Richter, Mr. Olsen, Mrs. Anderson and Miss Larson to the play.
14. I write great poems but I am not very good at writing paragraphs.
15. Look put the books on that table over there.

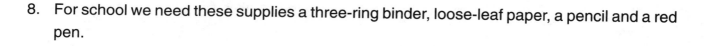

Personal Pronouns: *Introduction*

A **personal pronoun** is a word that takes the place of a noun. There are three types of personal pronouns: subject pronouns, object pronouns, and possessive pronouns.

Subject Pronouns

Subject pronouns take the place of the subject. The pronouns that are used as the subject are **I**, **we**, **you**, **he**, **she**, **it**, and **they**.

Example: *Michael* had the fastest time in the race.
He had the fastest time in the race.

Object Pronouns

Object pronouns are objects of the verb. The pronouns that are used as objects are **me**, **us**, **you**, **him**, **her**, and **it**.

Example: Jennifer gave *the pencil* to Scott.
Jennifer gave **it** to Scott.

* *Exception to the rule:* Following a verb like *is, was, are,* or *will be,* use **I**, **we**, **you**, **he**, **she**, **it**, or **they**.

The cook is *Louis.*
The cook is **he**. (He is the cook.)

Possessive Pronouns

Possesive pronouns show ownership. The pronouns that are used to show possession are **mine**, **his**, **hers**, **its**, **ours**, **yours**, and **theirs**.

Example: The best report was *Maria's.*
The best report was **hers.**

That is *my notebook.*
That is **mine.**

Name: ______________________________ Date: ______________

Personal Pronouns: *Exercise 1*

Directions: Proofread the following sentences carefully. Write "correct" in the blank next to the sentence if it is correct. Write the correct pronoun if it is incorrect.

1. Rodrigo carried the heavy boxes for she. ______________________
2. Them will be here soon to go to the party. ______________________
3. Candice said the fault was hers. ______________________
4. You can bring it into the room now. ______________________
5. Our is not the car we should be using. ______________________
6. Ralph and me are going to the movies on Saturday. ______________________
7. The librarian told them to be quiet in the library. ______________________
8. I don't think it was she. ______________________
9. Do you think this song would be good for Ann and I to sing? ______________________
10. Samantha and him are taking the notes for the whole class. ______________________
11. Its about time the leak in the ceiling was fixed. ______________________
12. I don't think your the winner of the election. ______________________
13. Did you ask them what they're doing after school? ______________________
14. Will Sophie give they the candy? ______________________
15. Beth and her will decorate for the school dance. ______________________

Name: ______________________________ Date: ____________________

Personal Pronouns: *Exercise 2*

Directions: Proofread and correct the following paragraph using proofreading marks.

At our school the sixth grade class has the opportunity to travel to Washington D.C. in the summer. Last year my class and me went. Us sixth graders visited the White House, the Smithsonian Institute, the Capitol, and the Vietnam Memorial. Them were all great sites. We rode on a plane to Washington and I and my best friend Sarah got to sit together. Her and I had a bunch of fun.

Us got to meet several Senators at the Capitol. Mr. Richards was our. We walked around and looked at the different offices. Him and our other senator have offices next to each other. Next we went to the White House. Their were guards in every room, but they were helpful and answered all the questions us had. Sarah and me walked around and tried to imagine what it was like to live they're.

The last place we went was the Vietnam Memorial. The big black wall was very impressive. Some people used paper and chalk to make rubbings of the names of there relatives. These relatives of their had died in the war. I don't know whose idea it was to build her but it was a good idea.

If your ever going to go on a school trip, I hope you go to Washington D.C. It was great.

Pronoun Antecedents: *Introduction*

An **antecedent** is the noun or pronoun that the pronoun refers to or replaces. All pronouns have antecedents. A pronoun must agree with its antecedent in number and gender. When the antecedent is singular, the pronoun must be singular; when the antecedent is plural, the pronoun must be plural. If the antecedent is male, the pronoun must be male; when the antecedent is female, the pronoun must be female. If the antecedent has no gender or is neutral, the pronoun must be neutral.

Examples: Frank is on the team. **He** wore his uniform for the picture.
Frank is the singular, male antecedent; *he* is the singular, male pronoun.

We have asked the teacher when the **test** would be given. The teacher told **us** **it** would be tomorrow.
We is the plural, neutral antecedent; *us* is the plural, neutral pronoun.
Test is the singular, neutral antecedent; *it* is the singular, neutral pronoun.

Jessie and Andrea took first and second place. **They** are very good tennis players.
Jessie and Andrea is the plural, neutral antecedent; *They* is the plural, neutral pronoun.

Anna has a library **card**. I know **it** is **hers** because her name is on **it**.
Anna is the singular, female antecedent; *hers* is the singular, female pronoun.
Card is the singular, neutral antecedent; *it* is the singular, neutral pronoun.

Everyone voted to buy the new projector, and **we** enjoyed the weekly movie day.
Everyone is the plural, neutral antecedent; *we* is the plural, neutral pronoun.

* The possessive adjectives **my**, **our**, **your**, **their**, **his**, **her**, and **its** must also agree in number and gender with the antecedents.

Name: ____ Date: ______________________

Pronoun Antecedents: *Exercise 1*

Directions: Read the following sentences carefully. Circle the correct pronoun for its antecedent.

1. Neither of the boys was happy when (his, their) dad told him he had to do chores.
2. Mike went to the grocery store; (he, she) bought bread and milk.
3. Wilma bought a new tennis racket. (Hers, Theirs, Its) was an expensive brand.
4. Ben and Sue played a new ball game; (it, they) was a lot of fun.
5. We had spaghetti for dinner; (she, it) was delicious.
6. Many hoped this would be the winning point. It was a disappointment to (they, them).
7. The elephant knelt down; (it, he) was still twice as tall as the trainer.
8. One of the dogs did tricks on command. (They, It) was a smart dog.
9. Erica gave everybody presents. (He, We) were happy to get (them, it).
10. How did people know (he, it, they) when the parade started?
11. One girl asked if (she, it, they) could answer the question.
12. She put her money in the bank. I don't know what to do with (it, mine, hers).
13. I put the books away. Did you wonder where (they, them) were?
14. Several of the cats were eating dinner. (They, It) each had a bowl.
15. Each man had a plan. Each thought (hers, his, its) was the best.

Name: ______________________________ Date: ________________

Pronoun Antecedents: *Exercise 2*

Directions: Rewrite the following paragraphs on the lines below. Correct any pronoun antecedent errors.

If you are going to have a pet, you need to know beforehand how to take care of it. Pets require a lot of time and effort if it is to live a healthy life. There are several things you must know in order to take care of any pet.

First you need to find a place for your pet to live. A dog will need a bed to sleep in and a place that they can go to get away from everyone if it wants. A cat will sleep wherever they want to. If you have a bird, you need to get a cage for them and make sure it is not in a drafty place.

Dogs, cats, and birds all need places for it to eat. A bird will eat in its cage unless you train it to eat somewhere else. Dogs and cats like to eat their meals somewhere where there isn't a lot of people who might bump into them.

All animals like to be exercised. If your pet just lies around the house all day, she will not be healthy, and they will get fat.

Make sure you take good care of your pets, and it will live with you for a long time.

Confusing Verbs: *Introduction*

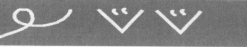

There are some verbs that have similar meanings, and they are often confused when writing. It is important to make sure when you are proofreading that you understand the meanings of these verbs and choose the correct one for the sentence.

Sit and Set

Sit means to be in a seated position.

I will **sit** in the garden and wait for you.

Set means to place something.

Please **set** the glass on the table.

Lie and Lay

Lie means to recline.

I think I will **lie** down and take a nap.

Lay means to place something.

Where did Jane **lay** my green sweater?

Rise and Raise

Rise means to move upward on its own.

The bread must **rise** in a warm place.

Raise means to lift.

At what time do we **raise** the flag?

There are many other verbs that have related meanings and are often confused as well, such as *learn* and *teach*, *can* and *may*, *let* and *left, leave* and *let,* and *borrow* and *lend.*

Name: ________________________________ Date: ________________

Confusing Verbs: *Exercise 1*

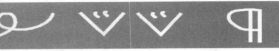

Directions: Read the following sentences carefully. Circle the correct verb to make the sentence correct.

1. Did you (sit, set) on the freshly painted park bench?
2. Denise was able to (rise, raise) her hand when the question was asked.
3. May I (borrow, lend) a dollar to buy my lunch?
4. Scott wanted to (learn, teach) how to play the piano, so he took lessons.
5. The bread dough had to sit in a warm place to (raise, rise).
6. Beth said she would (lend, borrow) Brian a sheet of paper for the quiz.
7. Please (sit, set) the groceries on the counter in the kitchen.
8. Pat was tired, so she wanted to (lay, lie) down and take a nap.
9. Lewis did not have to (left, leave) the soccer game early.
10. Jeff wanted to (learn, teach) Bill how to play the guitar.
11. Whose turn is it to (rise, raise) the flag at school?
12. Luis couldn't (learn, teach) the difficult dance steps.
13. Have you (let, left) your book bag on the bus?
14. Annie, don't (sit, set) on the antique chair.
15. Mona didn't (rise, raise) from her seat when the president came in.

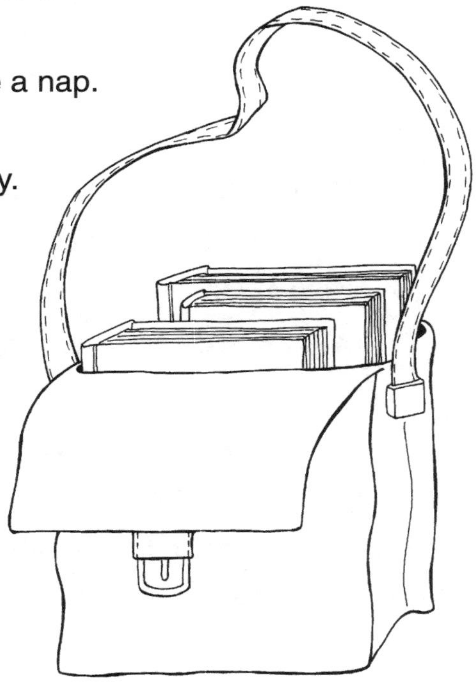

Name: ______________________________ Date: ____________________

Confusing Verbs: *Exercise 2*

Directions: Proofread and correct the following paragraph using proofreading marks.

I wanted to learn Bill a lesson about money. He always forgets his lunch money. Every day during history he comes up to me.

"Will you borrow me seventy-five cents for lunch?" Bill asks.

"Yes, but this is the last time," I reply.

"Oh, yeah, well see about that," he answers.

Then I sit the money on his desk, he takes it and puts it in his pocket, and he doesn't remember that he borrowed money from me. It is never the last time, though, because I give him the money each time. I am always afraid of what he will do if I say no. This is not helping Bill learn to be more responsible and it is hurting my savings.

Now I only take enough money for my lunch at school or I bring my lunch from home. The first day I did this, Bill came up to me during history and said, "Will you borrow me seventy-five cents for lunch?"

I answered in a very firm voice, "No, I only have enough for my lunch today."

Bill moaned, "You always leave me borrow money from you."

I stood my ground and said, "No." Then I waited for his reaction.

Bill looked at me; his arm rose up. I backed away, but he slapped me on the back anyway and said, "No problem, buddy." Then he set back down in his chair.

Guess I learned a lesson too.

Subject-Verb Agreement: *Introduction*

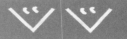

In writing, it is important to have the subject and the verb agree. Subjects and verbs can be singular or plural. If the subject is singular, then the verb must be singular. If the subject is plural, then the verb must be plural. If the subject is singular, an "s" is usually added to the verb.

Examples:

Kevin eats spaghetti with a spoon.	Singular subject, singular verb
Peaches are in season in the summer.	Plural subject, plural verb
Curt and Todd paint the house.	Plural subject, plural verb

Some sentences begin with "There is" or "There are." "There" is not the subject; the subject usually comes after the verb.

Examples:

There **is** a large **dog** outside.	Use *is* because *dog* is singular.
There **are** many **students** at our school.	Use *are* because *students* is plural.

When proofreading, make sure that there is both a subject and a verb. If either the subject or the verb is missing, then it is a sentence fragment.

Name: ______________________________ Date: ________________

Subject-Verb Agreement: *Exercise 1*

Directions: Proofread the following sentences carefully. Write correct in the blank below the sentence if it is correct. Rewrite the sentence if it is incorrect, correcting any errors in subject-verb agreement.

1. Jeff and Susan is going to be the speakers at the assembly.

   ____

2. Carmela are going to be the bridesmaid at her brother's wedding.

   ____

3. Either Miguel or Angela is going to run for class president.

   ____

4. Can you see if Tracey and Maria is coming over to our house?

   ____

5. Either Brian or Barbara are taking the dog for a walk.

   ____

6. Who run the tape recorder while we sing?

   ____

7. There is ten amendments to the Constitution that are called the Bill of Rights.

   ____

8. Jay and Elena thinks that it would be a good idea to start a newspaper.

   ____

9. Neither Sherry nor Lisa will be going to the movies tonight.

   ____

10. Mrs. Graham asked us to turn our papers in when we was finished.

    ____

Name: ______________________________ Date: ________________

Subject-Verb Agreement: *Exercise 2*

Directions: Rewrite the following paragraph on the lines below, correcting any errors in subject-verb agreement.

Next year I hopes to play the flute in the school orchestra. I has been taking lessons from Mrs. Elliot for three years. I think it is time for me to try out for the orchestra. I know I has had excellent lessons, and I have practiced every day. I still worries about standing in front of all the music teachers and playing my flute. It would be so easy to put my fingers in the wrong place or to holds my lip wrong. Neither my mom nor my dad think I will have any trouble at the audition, but I is not as sure. I still has a few months to practice and work at being brave. I hopes I gets to play in the school orchestra.

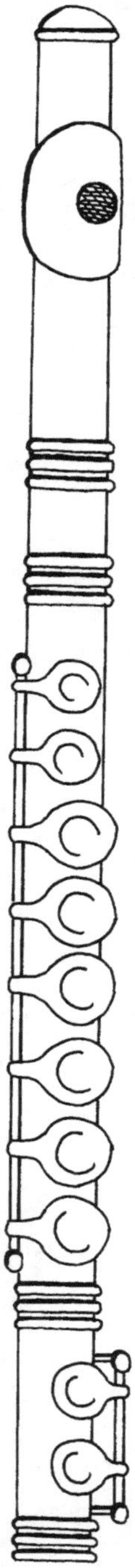

Compound Subjects and Indefinite Pronouns: *Introduction*

A **compound subject** is made up of two parts. When it is connected with the word "and," the subject is plural. When it is connected with the words "or" or "nor," it is plural if the nearest noun is plural and singular if the nearest noun is singular.

Examples

John and Jessica are going to play soccer after school.

John and Jessica is plural *are* is plural

Neither Jake nor **Carmen plays** on their team.

Carmen is singular *plays* is singular

Either this book or those **notebooks belong** to Andrea.

notebooks is plural *belong* is plural

Indefinite pronouns do not refer to any specific person, place, or thing, but refer generally to people, places, or things. They may take the place of a noun, but they sometimes don't have antecedents. Singular indefinite pronouns have singular verbs, and plural indefinite pronouns have plural verbs.

Examples

Both of the notebooks **are** Jeremy's.

Both is plural *are* is plural

Each of the boys **is** going to have a turn at bat.

Each is singular *is* is singular

Name: ______________________________ Date: ________________

Compound Subjects and Indefinite Pronouns: *Exercise 1*

Directions: Read the following sentences carefully. Circle the correct verb to make the sentence correct.

1. The baker and his assistants (starts, start) work early at the bakery.
2. Can Angie and Nick (take, takes) the dog for a walk?
3. Multiplication tables and division (require, requires) memorization.
4. Neither a basketball game nor tennis lessons (interests, interest) me today.
5. Either Jason or Luis (are, is) our starting pitcher tomorrow.
6. Your aunt and uncle (is, are) on their vacation in Mexico.
7. Colorful candies and a candle (decorates, decorate) the top of the cake.
8. Neither these boys nor that girl (wants, want) to walk to school in the cold.
9. The cat and her kittens (howl, howls) when they are hungry.
10. Either my brother or my dad (go, goes) to the doughnut shop on Saturday mornings.
11. Neither my sisters nor my mom (are, is) feeling very well today.
12. Mrs. Harrison's and Mrs. Morgan's classes (are, is) at the planetarium.
13. The bookcase shelves (is, are) full of books to read.
14. Eric and Beth (ride, rides) their bikes to school every day.
15. How many days (is, are) Karen and Marion going to be on vacation?

Name: ______________________________ Date: ____________________

Compound Subjects and Indefinite Pronouns: *Exercise 2*

Directions: Read the following sentences carefully. Underline the indefinite pronoun, and then circle the correct verb to make the sentence correct.

1. Laura uses pen and ink for her drawings, but others (use, uses) watercolors.
2. Does anyone (ride, rides) his or her bike to the park?
3. I hope neither of the kittens (are, is) out in the yard.

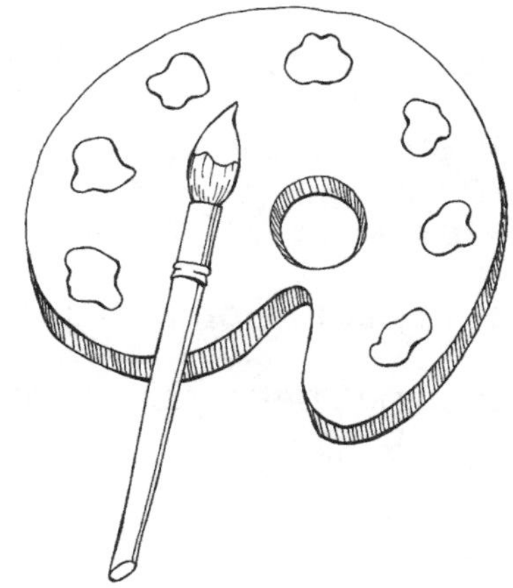

4. All of the cast of the play (bow, bows) at the final curtain call.
5. A few of the art students (helps, help) paint scenery.
6. Everybody (wants, want) a day with no homework.
7. Each of you (carry, carries) a bag of groceries into the house.
8. Something (is, are) missing from the puzzle.
9. Mrs. Evans said everyone (are, is) going on the field trip.
10. Neither of the girls (is, are) babysitting on Saturday.
11. Did you say both of the sweaters (is, are) Ramona's?
12. One of the puppies (are, is) sleeping in my lap.
13. I think someone (is, are) going to volunteer to give their speech first.
14. All of the students (cheer, cheers) at the football game.
15. Most of the puppies (sleep, sleeps) during the day.

Name: ______________________________ Date: ______________

Compound Subjects and Indefinite Pronouns: *Exercise 3*

Directions: Rewrite the following paragraph on the lines below, correcting any agreement errors.

Neither Jeff nor Ben are going out for the football team this year. Each of these boys has decided to play soccer instead. All of the soccer team is happy to have them join the team. The team feel that each of the boys has qualities that will help them to a championship season. Jeff has played soccer before when he was in second and third grade, but Ben has never played on a team. Many of the plays the boys will be learning is similar to plays in football. Some of the players is planning to help both boys becomes better acquainted with soccer and the rules.

Subject-Verb Arrangement: *Introduction*

In order to make papers and manuscripts more interesting, sentences may be switched around. For example, instead of having the subject come first and the verb come second, the verb will be first and the subject will be second.

Examples

The **cat hunts** for mice. — **Hunting** for mice **is** the **cat**.

Mr. Li talks to the students. — **Talking** to the students **is Mr. Li.**

Subjects and verbs are inverted when *here*, *there*, and *where* are used.

Examples

Here **are** the **books** you were looking for.

Where **is Uncle Steve**?

Subjects and verbs can be inverted when you write questions.

Examples

Are you going with Ben after school?

Is the **dog** or the **cat going** to the vet?

Make sure you check for subject-verb agreement.

Examples

On the table **were** several students' **notebooks**.

notebooks – subject, plural   *were* – verb, plural

Who **is** the **owner** of the dog?

owner – subject, singular   *is* – verb, singular

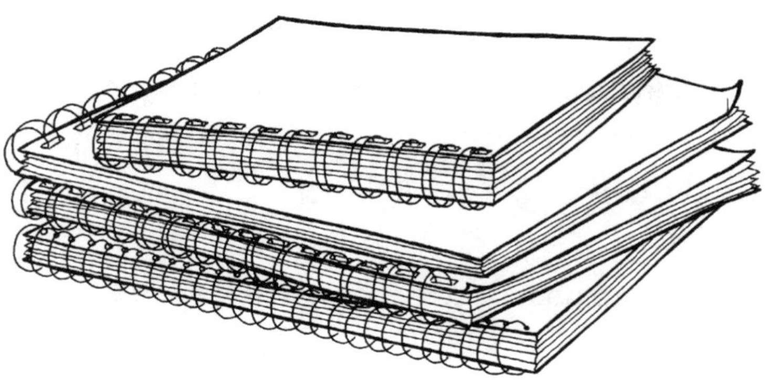

Name: ______________________________ Date: ________________

Subject-Verb Arrangement: *Exercise 1*

Directions: Proofread the following sentences carefully. Circle the correct verb for its subject to make the sentence correct.

1. Where (is, are) the book that goes on this shelf?
2. Under the porch (live, lives) a family of mice.
3. Here (is, are) the lists of overdue library books.
4. To the gym (go, goes) students who need schedule changes.
5. There (is, are) no one in the electronics department who can answer my question.
6. At the Mardi Gras celebration (was, were) many strange costumes.
7. The captain of the team (takes, take) the roster to the umpire.
8. (Was, Were) they late for school again?
9. There (is, are) better examples of evaporation than the one you chose.
10. (Is, Are) Jamal and Luisa the only ones going to the meeting?
11. Here (is, are) the best title for your book.
12. After practice (was heard, were heard) many heated arguments about the disputed call.
13. Under the microscope (appears, appear) small living creatures.
14. (Is, Are) a jonquil and a daffodil the same flower?
15. There (is, are) usually more people waiting in line for the movie.

Verb Tense: *Introduction*

When proofreading a paper, it is important to check **verb tense**. Is the paper written in the present, past, or future time? When you write your paper, it is important to keep the same tense throughout the paper.

Examples:

Present Tense – The girl *walks.*

Action that is happening now

Past Tense – The girl *walked.*

Action that happened in the past

Future Tense – The girl *will walk.*

Action that will happen in the future

Present Perfect Tense – The girl *has walked.*

Action that began in the past, but was completed in the present

Past Perfect Tense – The girl *had walked.*

Action that began in the past and was completed in the past

Future Perfect Tense – The girl *will have walked.*

Action that begins in the future and will be completed in the future

Name: ____ Date: ____________________

Verb Tense: *Exercise 1*

Directions: Proofread the following sentences carefully. Circle the correct verb tense to make the sentence correct.

1. In 1861, the North and South (starts, started) a civil war.
2. By the end of the day, Mike had (cleaned, cleans) his room.
3. Scott (participate, had participated) in every spelling bee.
4. If you eat this one too, you (eats, will have eaten) all of my birthday treats.
5. Jonathan (has picked, pick) enough apples for a pie.

6. Matt (looked, look) in every classroom for his books.
7. Last night we (make, made) decorations for the school dance.
8. Phil (will practice, practice) his piano piece many times.
9. As a joke, they (wears, wore) matching outfits all week.
10. Wendy (has known, knows) David for a long time.
11. Next month, Annie (was, will have been) in charge of the choir for two years.
12. Yesterday, Carol (wrote, write) a letter to the editor.
13. Our class (received, receive) a letter from the President of the United States.
14. Mrs. Garcia (help, helps) me understand my math.
15. We (tested, will test) all of the pens to see if they have ink.

Name: ______________________________ Date: ____________________

Verb Tense: *Exercise 2*

Directions: Rewrite the following paragraph on the lines below, correcting any errors in verb tense.

Storms is interesting weather phenomena. First an approaching storm created a large cloud. You can see the cloud in the sky as it got dark. Sometimes, when a storm is approaching, the temperature dropped. The storm gets closer, and the sky gets darker. When there was a storm, it can rain, hail, sleet, or even snow. Some storms caused a tornadoes. Tornadoes cause strong winds. The winds lasted for a few moments, but it can seem like hours. Storms have thunder and lightning. Even some tornadoes did have thunder and lightning. Storms were a powerful weather system.

____

____

____

____

____

____

____

____

____

____

____

____

Comparisons: *Introduction*

Comparison is shown by adding "er" to adjectives and adverbs when two things are compared and "est" when three or more things are compared.

Examples

I arrived at school **earlier** than you did.

Beth can yell **louder** than Stephanie.

Matt was the **happiest** boy in the classroom when he received the trophy.

Luis was the **youngest** player on the team.

Comparison is also shown with *more, most, less,* and *least.* These are used with adjectives and adverbs that are two or more syllables long.

Examples

My dog is **more beautiful** than your dog.

Andrew has the **most important** job on the dance committee.

Caroline went to the swimming pool **less often** this summer than last year.

Sometimes the comparative forms are spelled completely differently.

Examples

good:	better	best
much:	more	most
bad:	worse	worst

Name: ______________________________ Date: ________________

Comparisons: *Exercise 1*

Directions: Proofread the following sentences carefully. Write correct on the line below the sentence if it is correct. Rewrite the sentence if it is incorrect, correcting any errors in comparisons.

1. After school, I am having a sandwich and the most largest soda I can find.

   ____

2. I think the sense of smell is the stronger sense in animals.

   ____

3. Mrs. Ripley said that I had the goodest grade on the test of anyone in the class.

   ____

4. Mr. Nelson was the bravest person in the room when the snake slithered in.

   ____

5. Which baby is cuter, the one dressed in yellow or the one dressed in green?

   ____

6. Which of the three teachers gets to school the most early?

   ____

7. Even when the storm was at its baddest, our electrical power didn't go out.

   ____

8. One of the two plays is more popular than the other.

   ____

9. I think life in the 1950s was a simpler time than life today.

   ____

10. Taming wild animals must be the more dangerous job of any I have heard of.

   ____

Name: ______________________________ Date: ______________

Comparisons: *Exercise 2*

Directions: Rewrite the following paragraph on the lines below, correcting any errors in usage.

The sadder book I have ever read is *Old Yeller* by Fred Gipson. It is the story of a boy and his dog. There are many animal books that are interesting, and some are sad, but this is the goodest one I have read. Old Yeller comes to the cattle ranch and is adopted by Travis. They become the bestest of friends. They do everything together, and the dog watches over the family and the ranch. The love between the boy and his dog is the realest. The words on the pages made me think of my own dog and how I love it. There are parts in the book that you feel as if you are actually there with them. It is a sad book, and I cried more hard at the end.

Modifiers/Double Negatives: *Introduction*

When you are proofreading, you need to check for **modifiers**. Modifiers are adjectives, which modify nouns or pronouns, or adverbs, which modify verbs, adjectives, or other adverbs.

Examples

The **bright sun** shone on the lake.

The adjective is *bright*, which modifies the noun *sun.*

The sun **shone brightly** on the lake.

The adverb is *brightly*, which modifies the verb *shone*.

Watch for linking verbs as you proofread. There should be an adjective after the linking verb to connect it to the noun.

Examples

The chocolate cake **tastes delicious**.	(not *deliciously*)
The temperature **felt warm**.	(not *warmly*)

Double Negatives

A common error found in writing is the double negative. As you proofread, check for places where the adverb *not* is used. Look to make sure there isn't another word that also means "not."

Examples

Double negative:	Angela **didn't** do **nothing** wrong.
Correct:	Angela **didn't** do **anything** wrong.
Correct:	Angela **did nothing** wrong.
Double negative:	We **never** get to do **nothing**.
Correct:	We **never** get to do **anything**.
Correct:	We get to do **nothing**.

Name: ______________________________ Date: ______________

Modifiers: *Exercise 1*

Directions: Proofread the following sentences carefully. Circle the correct modifier to make the sentence correct. Underline the word the modifier modifies.

1. Our sailboats drifted (quiet, quietly) across the pond.
2. You appear (happy, happily) on this early morning.
3. Our music group sang (bad, badly) today during rehearsal.
4. Maggie yelled (loud, loudly) at her brother.
5. If we walk (real, really) quickly, we can get home before my brother.
6. Our book club meets (regular, regularly), even during the summer.
7. Did you open the door (cautious, cautiously)?
8. Apples and oranges are a (good, well) source of vitamins.
9. I (happy, happily) ate the last piece of chocolate cake.
10. Carrie was (complete, completely) honest when she talked with the teacher.
11. Last night the band played really (good, well) during the performance.
12. Do you think this music is too (slow, slowly) for the start of the pep rally?
13. The artist used (beautiful, beautifully) colors to paint the picture.
14. Do you think that extreme sports will be (real, really) popular?
15. Amanda read the poem (beautiful, beautifully) to the audience.

Name: ______________________________ Date: ____________________

Modifiers: *Exercise 2*

Directions: Rewrite the following paragraph on the lines below, correcting any errors in the use of modifiers.

Students who practice their musical instruments do good in their recitals. If you don't practice, you will play bad. The people sitting at the recital will think the time is passing real slowly if they have to listen to students who don't know the right notes to play. You can tell the students who are confidently. They come on the stage and sit careful on the edge of the chair and wait for the conductor to give them a signal. A student who is not prepared fumbles through his or her music and tries not to make eye contact with the conductor. It is much better to practice, so when you have a recital, you will feel confident, and the audience will enjoy your performance.

Name: ______________________ Date: ______________

Double Negatives: *Exercise 1*

Directions: Proofread the following sentences carefully. Write correct on the line below the sentence if it is correct. Rewrite the sentence if it is incorrect, correcting any double negatives.

1. There wasn't hardly enough food in the box to feed the dog.

   ____

2. We don't want no extra people on the decoration committee.

   ____

3. Do you want anything from the grocery store?

   ____

4. None of them had nothing to help fix up the playground equipment.

   ____

5. There wasn't no money left to pay for the food for the party.

   ____

6. The splinter was so small, you could hardly see it.

   ____

7. The information Karen and Suzy found for their report wasn't no good.

   ____

8. Have you ever eaten chocolate-covered grasshoppers?

   ____

9. Weren't none of the hockey players on the ice when you got to the arena?

   ____

10. I have never learned how to paint with watercolors.

    ____

Name: ______________________________ Date: ______________

Double Negatives: *Exercise 2*

Directions: Rewrite the following paragraph on the lines below, correcting any errors in the use of double negatives.

There hasn't hardly been a week at school better than last week. We didn't have no tests in any of our classes. There really wasn't scarcely any homework either. We had two assemblies during the week, too. One was a musical production, and one was a pep rally for our basketball team. During the one for the musical production, we didn't do nothing except sit and listen to the singing and dancing. They really did a nice job. Afterwards, the music teacher told us we should think about joining the choir when we go to high school. I don't think she meant me, because I don't have no talent. During the assembly for the basketball team, we did cheers and yells and listened to how good they had played during the year. I really like weeks when we don't have nothing to do.

Capitalization: *Introduction*

Capitalized letters are used to show that certain words and certain word groups are important. Capitalize words at the beginning of a sentence. Capitalize all proper nouns and adjectives. Capitalize titles of people and relatives. Capitalize holidays, important events, and periods of history.

Examples

Beginning of a sentence	**W**here are you going?	**I** am late.
Proper nouns	**B**enjamin **F**ranklin	**F**rance
Proper adjectives	**A**merican	**S**panish
Titles of people and relatives	**A**unt Barbara	**C**olonel James
	President George Bush	

Hint: Don't capitalize mom, dad, uncle, grandfather, and so on, when used with a possessive pronoun.

We went to my **g**randfather's house for dinner.

My **m**om drove us to school.

Holidays	**M**other's **D**ay	**T**hanksgiving
Special events, periods of history	**E**lection **D**ay	**D**ark **A**ges

Capitalize the first letter of all important words in the title of a book. Book titles are also underlined when handwritten. Book titles are printed in italics when they appear in printed material.

	Old **Y**eller	**D**iary of a **Y**oung **G**irl
	Old Yeller	*Diary of a Young Girl*
Abbreviations of proper nouns	**S**un.	**M**r.
Titles of specific events	**W**orld **S**eries	**R**ose **B**owl
Planets and heavenly bodies	**V**enus	**J**upiter
Names of specific planes, trains, and ships (also underlined or italicized)	**N**autilus	**A**ir **F**orce **O**ne
Specific regions	I live in the **N**orth.	We like the **E**ast.

Name: ______________________________ Date: ______________

Capitalization: *Exercise 1*

Directions: Proofread the following sentences carefully. Mark the letters that need to be capitalized with the correct proofreading symbol.

1. I live at 2214 maine st.
2. Do you think mrs. brown and mrs. everly will chaperone the party?
3. athens is the capital of what country?
4. The title of the book is *how to maintain and repair bicycles.*
5. The weatherman said that there would be twelve inches of snow in buffalo, new york.
6. Ben told the class that president bush was living in the white house.
7. I am supposed to meet melissa at the corner of oak and spring streets.
8. Was thomas jefferson the third president?
9. Do jim and shelly have practice on monday or tuesday?

10. my dog rusty sleeps in the laundry room.
11. Sonja and lester are going to a world series game in chicago.
12. Mr. nelson teaches math, history, and english at our school.
13. I would like to visit london, england, and rome, italy.
14. John Adams and Benjamin Franklin worked on the declaration of independence.
15. Steven is going to the strike and spare bowling alley after school today.

Name: ______________________________ Date: ________________

Capitalization: *Exercise 2*

Directions: Proofread the following paragraph carefully. Use the correct symbols to show letters that should be capitalized or letters that should be lower case.

My aunt and I went to the art museum to see the exhibit of monet paintings. I was supposed to go on a field trip with my Art class to the Museum, but I was sick that day and missed it. aunt barbara said that she would take me when I was well. We rode the train from the suburbs to downtown chicago. It was great to look out the window and see all the scenery flying by. The Train Station was just like it looks on TV with people rushing by on their way to work. At the Museum there was so much to see. We looked at several other exhibits before we went in to the monet area, where the paintings were hung on the walls. There were benches where you could sit and study the paintings. Some of the artists' paintings looked like my younger Sister had painted them. Others were so beautiful, I didn't want to leave. But the monet exhibit was the best of all; I thought I could stay in that room forever. I whispered to aunt Barbara, "don't you wish you could paint like that? I know i do." On the train ride home, I looked out the window and saw the scenery the way monet must have looked at it, not just flying by, but in blues and greens and yellows. I always thought History was my favorite subject, but now I think it's Art.

Colloquialisms: *Introduction*

When you are writing a paper, book, or manuscript, it is important to use formal English, not informal English. Formal English is the English that is used most often in the business world. Informal English is the English you use with your friends or relatives. Because you are used to hearing friends talk informally, it is difficult to tell when something doesn't sound right and should be changed to formal English.

Colloquialisms are words and phrases that you use with your friends. Words like *dunno* or *gonna* are slang words that shouldn't be used in your writing for school. When you say that something is *neat* or *cool,* you are also using colloquialisms.

As you write, be very careful not to use slang in your paper unless you are writing direct quotations. Make sure as you proofread a paper that you look at more than whether or not something sounds right.

Examples:

Informal	The carnival ride was *cool.*
Formal	The carnival ride was *exciting.*
Informal	I *dunno* the answer to that question.
Formal	I *don't know* the answer to that question.
Informal	He said that? *No way!*
Formal	He said that? *That's unbelievable!*

Name: ______________________________ Date: ________________

Colloquialisms: *Exercise 1*

Directions: Proofread the following sentences carefully. Rewrite the sentences on the lines below, using formal English.

1. I saw the neatest outfit on sale at the mall yesterday.

   ____

2. Old man Morris always gives me the creeps.

   ____

3. Jonathan was just like all the other little rug rats.

   ____

4. I shouldn'ta been out later than my curfew.

   ____

5. I gotta get home before dinner tonight.

   ____

6. I received ten bucks for cleaning the yard; I am in the money now.

   ____

7. Do you think that school oughta start an hour later?

   ____

8. Winter is always cold and icky.

   ____

9. George Washington was an awesome president.

   ____

10. Where did you find that way cool bicycle?

    ____

Name: ______________________________ Date: ______________

Colloquialisms: *Exercise 2*

Directions: Rewrite the following paragraph on the lines below, correcting any errors in the use of colloquialisms.

Wow! I saw the coolest thing today. My buddy and I were out, just hanging around, when a fire truck went screaming by us. We thought that was awesome, so we hopped on our bikes and went high-tailing after it. That truck could really move; it was hard to keep up with it. I bet we followed that buggy for at least eight blocks. The firemen were hanging on the back of the truck, and it looked like a couple more guys were riding inside, plus there was the driver and the guy in the passenger's seat. Jason, my pal, wanted to stop after a couple of blocks, but I said no way, we weren't going to let this one get away. I peddled my bike with all my heart. Finally, the firetruck turned a corner, and we heard it stop. By the time we got around the corner, the truck had just pulled into the station. I thought it was going to go somewhere neat, like a huge fire, but it had just been out on a practice run. I wasn't blue though, because the firemen let us look at the truck while they put things away. No problem, we still thought it was far out.

Name: ______________________________ Date: ______________

Proofreading Review: *Exercise 1*

Directions: Proofread the following paragraph for misspelled or misused words. Circle each misspelled or misused word, and write the correct word on one of the lines below.

My favoritest place to visit is the zoo in our town. It is located not to far from my house, so I can walk there whenever I chose. Today, I started my visit at the lion house. While I was their, I watched the great yellow cats prowl around they're outside enclosure. Next, I visited the monkeys, who entertained me by running around and climbing trees. Then I choose to stop and feed the ducks some peaces of bred that I had brought along. I sat very quiet, and soon a mother duck and her ducklings came up and ate from my hand. I finished my visit by going to the seal pond. Its fun to watch them sun themselves on the rocks or swim in their deep, green pond. After a while, I looked at my watch and realized it was time to go home. Today at the zoo was the best day yet!

1. ______________ 2. ______________

3. ______________ 4. ______________

5. ______________ 6. ______________

7. ______________ 8. ______________

9. ______________ 10. ______________

Name: ______________________________ Date: ____________________

Proofreading Review: *Exercise 2*

Directions: Proofread the following paragraph for misspelled or misused words. Circle each misspelled or misused word, and write the correct word on one of the lines below.

After our school trip to the bank, I think that being a bank teller is the most funnest and exciting job. A bank teller does many different things in the bank. He or she handles transactions for customers, such as deposits and withdrawls. A teller also takes cutomers loan payments and helps them fix any problems they have in there accounts.

Some bank tellers also work in the drive-through to help customers who do not want to get out of their cars. Being in the drive-through is a more fast-paced area then working in the lobby. They're can be many different lanes of cars, and the teller has to be sure to keep them all straight.

Working in a bank can also be very interesting, because it allows you to meat and talk to different people every day. The other people who work at the bank are also very nice. They took us on a tour of the vault and let many of the students use the coin counter to add up there change.

Our trip to the bank was very unformative, and I think that I wood like to work at a bank.

1. ____________________ 2. ____________________

3. ____________________ 4. ____________________

5. ____________________ 6. ____________________

7. ____________________ 8. ____________________

9. ____________________ 10. ____________________

Name: ______________________________ Date: ______________

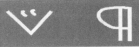

Proofreading Review: *Exercise 3*

Directions: Proofread the following paragraph for misspelled or misused words. Circle each misspelled or misused word, and write the correct word on one of the lines below.

One day, my dad and I decided to plant a garden in are backyard. My dad has done a lot of gardening, and he said he would learn me. We began by bying packages of seeds from a gardening store down the street from our house. We picked out carrots, lettuce, daisies, and marigolds. After changing into old close, we dug up a section of dirt in the backyard. Then I poked holes in the soft, brown dirt and dropped one seed into each whole. When all the seeds had been planted, I covered them up with dirt and watered them well with the hose. I make labels for each of the different plants to show were each type of seed had been planted. Every day, I check on the garden to make sure there are know weeds growing and that the plants are being watered. In a few weaks, we will have fresh vegetables to eat and flowers to share with our friends. Its very easy to start a garden.

1. ______________________ 2. ______________________

3. ______________________ 4. ______________________

5. ______________________ 6. ______________________

7. ______________________ 8. ______________________

9. ______________________ 10. ______________________

Name: ______________________________ Date: ______________

Proofreading Review: *Exercise 4*

Directions: Proofread the following paragraph for misspelled or misused words. Circle each misspelled or misused word, and write the correct word on one of the lines below.

There are several things you should do to study for a test. The first things you need are a positive atitude and a quite place to do you're studying. You may think its nice to study with the radio or TV on, but you are really not giving the subject your studying enough attention. The next thing to do is to review each chapter that will be covered by the test to see what important things or stressed in that chapter. It is also helpful to read over any notes from the chapters, highlighting important words, names, and dates. Next, try looking at just the highlighted words and quiz yourself. Be sure to look up any knew vocabulary words that you are unsure of or that your teacher said were important. It is also essential to go to the end of each chapter to answer any review questions. Write down the answers; then look at the answers to see if you can tell what the question is. When you feel you can answer the questions without having to look up the answers or refer to your notes, you are already to take the test. If you study careful before a test, you are on your way to recieving a good grade!

1. ____________________ 2. ____________________

3. ____________________ 4. ____________________

5. ____________________ 6. ____________________

7. ____________________ 8. ____________________

9. ____________________ 10. ____________________

Name: ______________________________ Date: ______________

Proofreading Review: *Exercise 5*

Directions: Proofread the following paragraph for misspelled or misused words. Circle each misspelled or misused word, and write the correct word on one of the lines below.

This summer my friends and I went to a Renaissance Fare held in are town. It was very exciting. It was held in a large open field, and all around it were sit up little booths and tents. Many of the people who were visiting were dressed in medieval clothing. The woman wore long dresses and pointy hats with veils on their heads. Many of the men wore tights and carryed swords. I looked at all the booths that were selling things first. There was one that sold handmade jewlery and another that sold dryed floral wreaths for people to wear on their heads. I stopped at a booth celling food and bought a giant turkey leg to eat for lunch. In the afternoon there was a jousting tournament to watch. Knights on horses charged down the field and tried to knock each other off there horses. There was also a demonstration of sword fighting. We really enjoyed our visit too the Renaissance Fair.

1. ______________________ 2. ______________________

3. ______________________ 4. ______________________

5. ______________________ 6. ______________________

7. ______________________ 8. ______________________

9. ______________________ 10. ______________________

Name: ______________________________ Date: ______________

Proofreading Review: *Exercise 6*

Directions: Proofread the following paragraph for capitalization errors. Circle each error, and write the correct word on one of the lines below.

This summer my Mom and Dad took my brother and me to London, england. One of the most exciting things I got to do for the first time was to ride in an airplane. We had to arrive at the Airport a few hours early, so we could check in our bags and have our tickets stamped. The airport was very large, and we had to walk a long way to get to the plane. I was surprised at how small the plane was inside. Everyone had to sit very close together; there was not much room to stretch our legs. Then the plane started rushing down the runway, and suddenly we were in the air. The flight was very long, but we tried to keep busy to make the time pass more quickly. Mom and dad watched a movie for part of the flight. My Brother and I played cards. We also were able to sleep for a while with pillows that were provided by the Airline. Then the Flight Attendant served us dinner on little plastic trays. The landing was very exciting as well. As we got closer to london, we could look out the window and see all sorts of little towns and buildings. I really enjoyed my first plane trip.

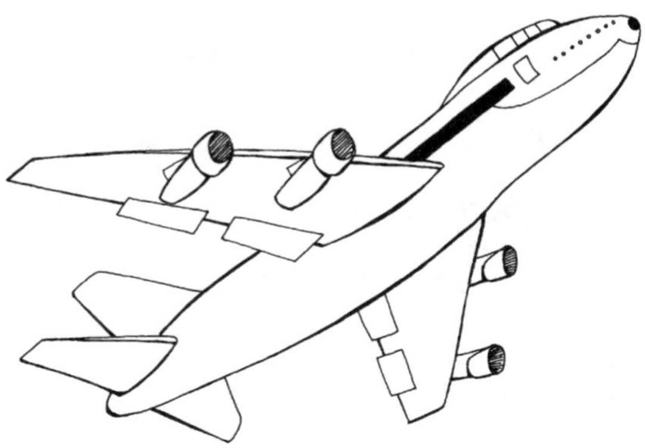

1. ______________ 2. ______________

3. ______________ 4. ______________

5. ______________ 6. ______________

7. ______________ 8. ______________

9. ______________ 10. ______________

Name: ______________________________ Date: ______________

Proofreading Review: *Exercise 7*

Directions: Proofread the following paragraph for capitalization errors. Circle each error, and write the correct word on one of the lines below.

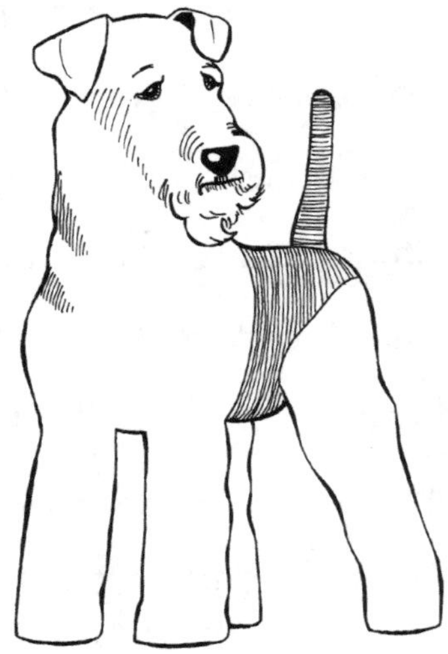

Today we got a new dog. We have never had a dog before, only cats. My Mom and dad told my Sister and me to do some research, so we could decide which kind of dog we would like to get. First, we went to the Pet Store to look at the different types of dogs. We also read many books about different breeds to see what type of dog would be best for our family. We didn't want one that was too loud and barked too much, but we didn't want one that was too quiet and didn't want to play either. We read about Labrador retrievers, Collies, Poodles, and Airedales.

Next, we decided to go to see the Breeder who lives in the next town. On the way to pick out our perfect puppy, everyone was excited. After checking out all the puppies, we decided to get an airedale puppy. We knew this was the perfect dog for us; he was small and bouncy and looked like he would be a fun addition to our family. We took our puppy home and named him rusty. We are all very happy with the new member of our Family.

1. ______________________ 2. ______________________

3. ______________________ 4. ______________________

5. ______________________ 6. ______________________

7. ______________________ 8. ______________________

9. ______________________ 10. ______________________

Name: ____________________ Date: ____________

Proofreading Review: *Exercise 8*

Directions: Proofread the following story, write any colloquialisms in the first column below. In the second column, write the word or phrase in formal English.

I caught a ride with my mom for my first day at Adams Middle School. Since I was the new guy, it was kinda scary because I had to make new friends and meet new teachers. But it went o.k. for the first day, and I figured that I'd catch on in no time.

The next day I was so jittery that my mind went blank. I forgot what my schedule was; I was so embarrassed because I couldn't even find my next class. A teacher saw me wandering in the hall after the bell had rung and helped me find my class. He even gave me a school map. I never did catch his name, but he was one awesome guy!

I am now more than halfway through the school year. My teachers are cool, and I have a group of buddies to hang out with. I can find my classes, no problem. But I will always remember the teacher who helped me at the beginning of the school year.

1. ____________________ ____________________
2. ____________________ ____________________
3. ____________________ ____________________
4. ____________________ ____________________
5. ____________________ ____________________
6. ____________________ ____________________
7. ____________________ ____________________
8. ____________________ ____________________
9. ____________________ ____________________
10. ____________________ ____________________
11. ____________________ ____________________
12. ____________________ ____________________
13. ____________________ ____________________
14. ____________________ ____________________

Name: ______________________________ Date: ____________________

Proofreading Review: *Exercise 9*

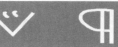

Directions: Proofread the following story, using the correct proofreading marks and making changes where necessary.

My favorite season of the year is Summer. I start thinking about it as soon as the snow starts to melt and I feel like the days are getting a little bit warmer. Summer is a time when the swimming are pools open and every one can be out riding its bike or playing tennis. It is hot and humid during the summer where I live but that is great because you can were shorts sandles and tank tops and the sun beats down on you. It is great to soak up the warmth after the cold winter. Summer is the time of year when kids are out of school and have three months to do all the things they have dreamed about doing during the winter. They can do whatever they please. If they want to participate in sports they can, if they want to sit under a tree in the shade and watch the clouds roll by they can do that too. Summer is the time you can spend with your friends but you can also spend with you family. Its a great time to go on a vacation with your family and visit relatives or a place you have never been before. Summer is the greatest and funnest time.

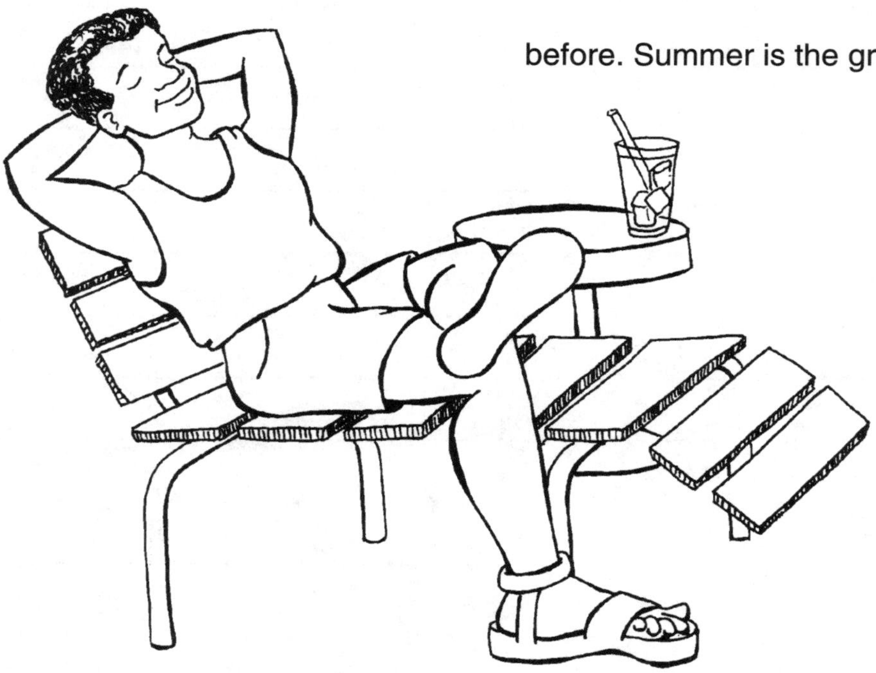

Name: ______________________________ Date: ____________________

Proofreading Review: *Exercise 10*

Directions: Proofread the following story, using the correct proofreading marks and making changes where necessary.

On our family vacation last year, we traveled to mississippi and visited the gulf coast. It was my first ever trip to the ocean. It was a very long drive to get to the gulf from our house. When we got there we stayed at a hotel that was right on the beach, we could walk stragight out of our hotel room and be on the sand. We spent nearly every day on the beach. The water was very warm and a beautiful blue green color. My brother and I would spend our time paddeling in the water or building sand castles on the beach. We would also walk up and down the sand after the tide had gone out, looking for shells. We found a hole bunch of different kinds. One day my Mom and Dad rented a sailboat and took us out on to the Gulf, we had a great time. A sailboat can go very fast and the boat was rocking so much that my brother got sick! i had the funnest time on our vaca-tion to the beach.

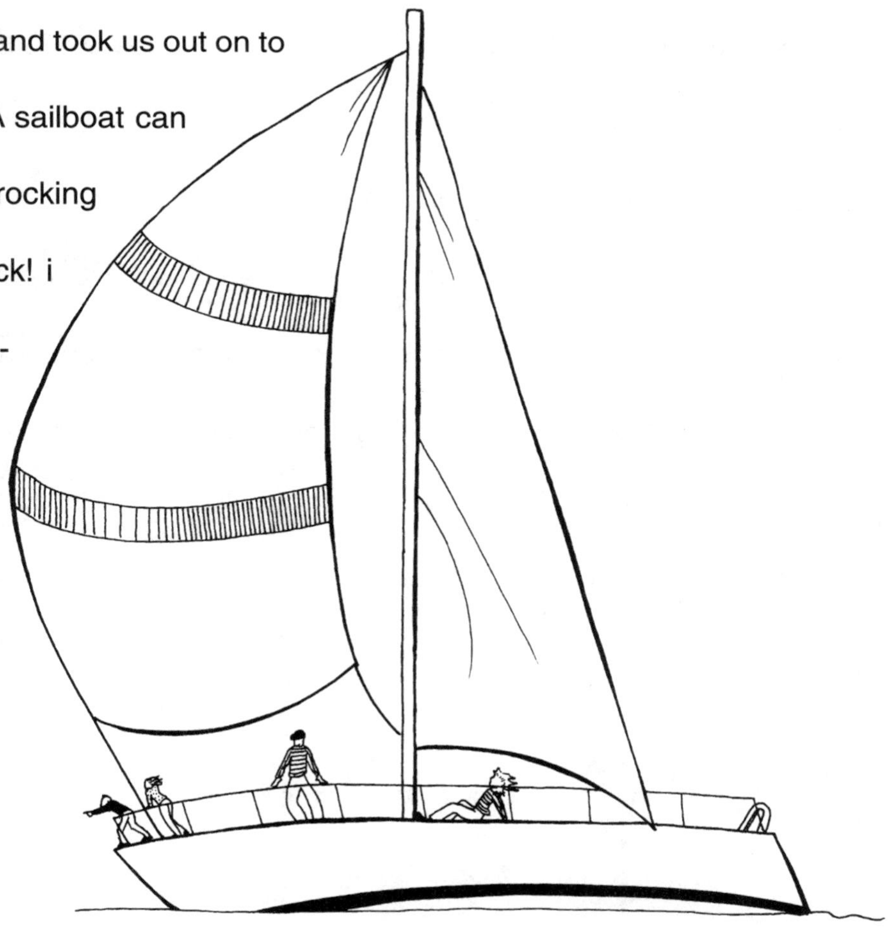

Name: ______________________________ Date: ________________

Proofreading Review: *Exercise 11*

Directions: Proofread the following story, using the correct proofreading marks and making changes where necessary.

I think that a cat makes the very best sort of pet. We have a cat named Tigger. We gets him from the Humane Society when he was just a kitten. When he was little he was such a cute little cat! He was small with orange fur and a little pink nose. Now that he is more older, he has grown huge. When he was small his favorite trick was to set on a chair and wait for our dog to come by so he could jump on the dogs back. I would yell, Look out! Sometimes that would get the dog to move. Tigger is much older now, so he is not as active. What he really likes to do now is to sit outside in the sun. He is scared of birds, so he like it if someone will sit outside with him. He also likes to eat the grass; really, he likes to eat anything. We feed him dry cat food, but he loves it if he gets a tin of moist food. He gets real excited if someone uses the can opener, even if there is no food for him. Tigger si a silly cat but we love him anyway.

Name: ______________________________ Date: ____________________

Proofreading Review: *Exercise 12*

Directions: Proofread the following story, using the correct proofreading marks and making changes where necessary.

My favorite thing to do on a warm summers day is to go on a picnic. There are a nice empty feild near our house with lots of large trees to sit under. It is the perfect place to sit and eat. The first thing to do is to pack a lunch in a basket. I usually brung a tuna sandwich, a hardboiled egg apples cookies and some lemonade. I pack it all up with plaits napkins and cups. I also bring a blanket to sit on and a book to read. Then I all ready to go. It is just an short walk from our house to the field. After searching all around you find just the right place to sit. It is flat and grassy and they're is plenty of shade from a nearby tree. I spread out the blanket and unpack my lunch. The food just seems to taste gooder when its ate outside. After eating all my lunch I lay on my blanket and reed my book. Then when it starts to get dark, I pack up all my things and head for home.

Name: ____ Date: ______________________

Proofreading Review: *Exercise 13*

Directions: Proofread the following story, using the correct proofreading marks and making changes where necessary.

Halloween is my favoritest holiday of the whole year. I spend many weeks thinking about what I am going to dress up as. I also make my own costume, with some help from my mom. This year I decided to go as an indian princess. My mom and me made a tan dress and embroidered geometric designs on it so it looked like an indian outfit. I also made an indian headdress and I took some black yarn and braided it to make two long black braid. Next I attached the braids to the head-dress. When Halloween came I wore my costume to school for our annual Halloween costume contest. This year I won second prize. That night after dinner my younger brother and me went out trick or treating to every house in our neighberhood. My favorite treats are the little candy bars, my Brother likes chewing gum. Even though Halloween has just ended, I am all ready thinking of a new costume for next year.

Name: ______________________________ Date: ____________________

Proofreading Review: *Exercise 14*

Directions: Proofread the following story, using the correct proofreading marks and making changes where necessary.

My Grandfather came over to our house today to help my mother and I bake cookies. We are going to use his special recipie and give them to my Father as a birthday present.

First we went to the grocery stor to buy all the eingredients. We had decided to make chocolate chip cookies because those are his most favoritest ones. We got a grocery cart and filled it up with flour a carton of eggs a bag of sugar chocolate chips and a container of vanilla. We also got my Grandfathers special ingredient: toffee pieces.

After getting home again and unpacking all our ingredients we got out our our mixer and started making the cookies. First we creamed butter and sugar and vanilla, then we added the eggs. When the mixture was smooth and creamy we added flour, salt, and baking soda. Then we stirred in the chocolate chips and the toffee pieces. We had preheated are oven, so we were all set to drop the spoonfuls of cookie dough on the cookie sheet. I like to et the cookie dough even better than the cookies.

When the cookies were done baking and had cooled off we put them in a pretty box decorated with balloons and ties it with a blue ribbon. When we gave it to my Dad, he said, "The cookies are delicious and one of the the best presents I've ever got!

Name: ______________________________ Date: ________________

Proofreading Review: *Exercise 15*

Directions: Proofread the following story, using the correct proofreading marks and making changes where necessary.

Last year me and my family took a trip to my grandparents house. Since they lived very far a way we decided to take the train. When the day to leave finally came I packed a suitcase and a extra bag with books and a CD player for the trane trip. Wehn we got on the train the first thing we did was pick out our seats. I was able to get one near the window wear I could watch the scenry go by. After a few hours my Brother and I went to the snack car on the train and bought something for dinner. There were all sort of chips candy and hot sandwiches available. I then went over to the observation car, this was a part of the train that had had big long windows so passengers could see the countryside. I sat for awhile and watchd farms and small towns go bye. After a few more hours we pulled into the station in my Grandparents town. I think riding the train is an awesome way to travel?

Name: ______________________________ Date: ____________________

Proofreading Review: *Exercise 16*

Directions: Proofread the following story, using the correct proofreading marks and making changes where necessary.

Today I started an after-school job of delivering newspapers for our local newspaper. It is a very cool job because I am earning extra money. But it is also a lot of work.

The first thing I do when I get home are to count the number of newspapers that the newspaper office dropped off at my house. I want to make sure that they're are enough to fill all my customers orders. Then I fold each newspaper in half and put it in my large canvas bag. When I am delivering the sunday paper the bag can get very heavy. Since my newspaper route is pretty small I can ride my bike around two deliver the papers. It is important to put everyone paper in the correct spot. Some want it in there mailboxes and others want it put on their front porches. At the end of the month I go around to each customer and collect the newspaper payment and take it down to the newspaper office. I very much enjoy my new after-school job, but its a lot of responsibility.

Name: ______________________________ Date: ____________________

Proofreading Review: *Exercise 17*

Directions: Proofread the following story, using the correct proofreading marks and making changes where necessary.

In the wintertime even though it is cold out and there is lots of snow their are many fun outdoor activites to do.

One of my favorite winter activities are skiing. I usually do both downhill and cross-coutnry skiing. It is fun to do downhill skiing because of the speed while going down the slopes. With cross-country the speed is slower but it gives you a chance to enjoy the winter scenery.

Sledding si also fun because it doesn't very much equipment and you can do it with a bunch of friends. All that is really needed is a hill and a sled.

The last fun winter activity is ice fishing. Its done by cutting a hole in a frozen lake an catching fish through the ice. It is an activity that requires a lot of patients.

Name: ______________________________ Date: ____________________

Proofreading Review: *Exercise 18*

Directions: Proofread the following story, using the correct proofreading marks and making changes where necessary.

My Dad got another job in a different town so were going to move to a new house. My Mom and Dad have all ready picked out our new house we have packed up all of our belongings. Today the moving truck came to transport all of our stuff to the new house. The movers make sure that all of our boxes were safely put in the truck. They also put blankets around all the furniture to keep it from getting damaged.

We folowed the moving van to the new house and watched while the movers unpacked all of our boxes. The new house is really cool with a great big yeard with a swing set. While we were unpacking our boxes two guys from down the street that are my age stopped by to say hello. They were real freindly and I think we will all be good buddies. Even though its kinda scary to move I think I will like are new house.

Name: ______________________________ Date: ________________

Proofreading Review: *Exercise 19*

Directions: Proofread the following story, using the correct proofreading marks and making changes where necessary.

For someone who has never seen white flakes that fall to the gound it might be hard to imagine. It really truly is a very neat thing to see. At times though winter can be a very dangerous seson. For people who haven't experience winter let me tell you something of what it is like.

For some states or even countries there really is no change from fall to winter but in my state of Illinois there definitely is. The first thing you start to notice is the change in tempaerature. Its not that one day its 70 degrees and the next day its 20 degrees. Its not that dramatic. But the temperature does fall and it gets colder and colder starting in November. That is just the beginning. There are more to winter than just cold weather.

After the cold weather comes bad wether begins. Usually its just snow but there can also be rain and sleet and freezing rain. This causes cars to wrecks and schools to close. Sometimes there is so much snow that people can't even leave their homes. Thats when it's really awesome. Weather people try to predict what the weather will be in the winter but its a difficult job to try to figure out when the weather is so unpredictable.

Winter can be a beautiful season and people can have a lot of fun but When the bad weather comes it is also very dangerous.

Name: ______________________________ Date: ________________

Proofreading Review: *Exercise 20*

Directions: Proofread the following story, using the correct proofreading marks and making changes where necessary.

Making a sandwich is an easy and fun thing to do. You can fix a sandwich for a snack or for your lunch. Here are you're easy directions.

First you gotta wash your hands with water and soap for about sixty seconds. This is to avoid any contact with germs. Then get out the ingreidients you want to use for you're sandwich. You also need to get out the utensils that youll need to make the sandwich.

To begin take two slices of bread and lightly toast them in the toaster. Wehn the bread are toasted take it out of the toaster and place it on a napkin or plate. Spread mustard or ketchup or mayonaize on each piece of the bred. If you like put a little of each on the toast. Slice a tomato and put one or too slices on one piece of the bread. Take five slices of pickles and put them on top of the tomato. The next thing to put on your bread is the meat. You have a choice of beef, chicken, turkey are salami, put one or two slices on your sandwich. Top this off with a slice of cheese, either yellow or white cheese is good and sometimes people want both. Add some leafy green lettuce to the sandwich and put your second piece of toast on the sandwich. I hope your mouth is big enough to eat a sandwich like this.

Answer Keys

Proofreading — Punctuation – Commas: *Exercise 1*

Name: ______________________ Date: __________

Punctuation – Commas: *Exercise 1*

Directions: Proofread the following sentences carefully. Write correct in the blank below the sentence if it is correct. Rewrite the sentence if it is incorrect, adding commas where needed.

1. "Juan did you do your homework last night?" asked Angela.
   "Juan, did you do your homework last night?" asked Angela.
2. I had a banana an orange two carrots and a sandwich for lunch.
   I had a banana, an orange, two carrots, and a sandwich for lunch.
3. "Yes I think it would be a good idea to read the story together" said Mrs. Martinez.
   "Yes, I think it would be a good idea to read the story together," said Mrs. Martinez.
4. When I went to the ballgame I caught a fly ball.
   When I went to the ballgame, I caught a fly ball.
5. Laura will write the paper proofread it and then turn it in to the newspaper.
   Laura will write the paper, proofread it, and then turn it in to the newspaper.
6. "Ask for a paper, a pencil, and a book," said Mrs. Bloom.
   correct
7. Do you like roses daffodils mums or tulips?
   Do you like roses, daffodils, mums, or tulips?
8. Amy wanted to go to the movies but Beth wanted to play tennis.
   Amy wanted to go to the movies, but Beth wanted to play tennis.
9. Look there is a fox in the backyard.
   Look, there is a fox in the backyard.
10. I have a large dog, and I have a very small cat.
    correct

© Mark Twain Media, Inc., Publishers 5

Proofreading — Punctuation—Commas: *Exercise 2*

Name: ______________________ Date: __________

Punctuation—Commas: *Exercise 2*

Directions: Proofread the following paragraph carefully. Using the correct symbol, insert commas where needed.

On January 14, 2001, we had the biggest snowstorm in the history of our town. The snow was so deep, believe it or not, that it came up to my dad's chest. I think the only place that had more snow than our town was Buffalo, New York. Snow, even though it looks light, is very difficult to shovel when it is that deep. It was even too deep for our snow blower, but once we had taken off the top layer with a shovel, it was easier. My brother, sister, and I were all outside helping. One of the hardest things to do was to lift the shovel high enough to throw the next shovelful. One time, when I wasn't paying attention to what I was doing, I threw my shovel of snow, and it landed right on my sister, who was shoveling on the other side of the snow mound. With that much snow, you have to plan where you are going to put the stuff. If you plan it right, you can get a really big heap of snow in one spot, so later you can build a fort or use the hill to sled down. It is fun to be outdoors with all that snow, working with your family, but I like it when we are finished and come in for hot chocolate.

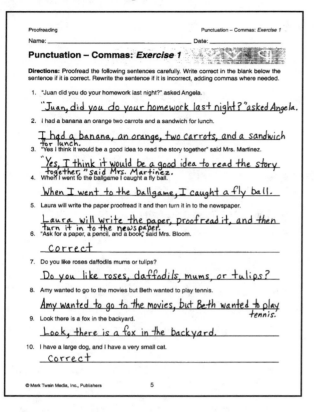

© Mark Twain Media, Inc., Publishers 6

Proofreading — Punctuation—Commas: *Exercise 3*

Name: ______________________ Date: __________

Punctuation—Commas: *Exercise 3*

Directions: Proofread the following paragraph carefully. Using the correct symbol, insert commas where needed.

"Mrs. Evans, will you please help me with question number six?" Caroline asked.

"I think you should ask one of the students in your group," answered Mrs. Evans.

That is how our math class works. We are given assignments each day to work on in math, and we work together in groups to solve the problems. Mrs. Evans told us this is the way many important problems are solved in the world.

Sometimes we pick our own groups. When we do, I like to be with Becky, Ben, and Allison. We are all friends. This doesn't always work out because we end up talking about other things and don't always get the problem done. If we were working on a world problem, this probably wouldn't be the best group for me to be with.

Other times Mrs. Evans puts us in a group. She will use numbers, eye color, age, or height to decide our groups. We never know what it will be. These groups usually work the best. We don't talk as much about other things, and we get more work done. Sometimes there are people who don't work at all, but Mrs. Evans said that happens with world problems too.

It would probably be best to look at the class, choose the people who work the hardest, and work with them. This would help me get my math problems solved. In the world, hopefully, that is what happens when problems are being solved.

© Mark Twain Media, Inc., Publishers 7

Proofreading — Punctuation—End Marks: *Exercise 1*

Name: ______________________ Date: __________

Punctuation—End Marks: *Exercise 1*

Directions: Proofread the following sentences carefully. Write correct in the blank below the sentence if it is correct. Rewrite the sentence if it is incorrect, adding periods where needed.

1. My appointment with Dr Jones is Thurs at 4 PM
   My appointment with Dr. Jones is Thurs. at 4 P.M.
2. On Tues I got a letter from St Louis, Missouri, where Mr Anderson lives
   On Tues. I got a letter from St. Louis, Missouri, where Mr. Anderson lives.
3. The bicycle race will start on Locust St at 10 AM and end at Spruce Ave
   The bicycle race will start on Locust St. at 10 A.M. and end at Spruce Ave.
4. Mrs Anderson and Mr Martin are the sponsors of the trip on Mon
   Mrs. Anderson and Mr. Martin are the sponsors of the trip on Mon.
5. J K Rowling writes the Harry Potter books
   J.K. Rowling writes the Harry Potter books.
6. Jan and Feb are the coldest months of the year.
   Jan. and Feb. are the coldest months of the year.
7. Ms Walker is going to meet me at 6 PM on Thursday
   Ms. Walker is going to meet me at 6 P.M. on Thursday.
8. The ABC Co will be opening its new store on Fri
   The ABC Co. will be opening its new store on Fri.
9. Dr Wong will be in surgery at the hospital on Maine St
   Dr. Wong will be in surgery at the hospital on Maine St.
10. Sen Long lives in Washington, DC, our nation's capital.
    Sen. Long lives in Washington, D.C., our nation's capital.

© Mark Twain Media, Inc., Publishers 9

Answer Keys

Proofreading Punctuation—End Marks: *Exercise 2*

Name: ______________________ Date: ____________

Punctuation—End Marks: *Exercise 2*

Directions: Rewrite the following paragraph on the lines below, using periods in the correct places.

Last week my mom made an appt for me at Dr Warner's office; he is an eye doctor. I had to get my eyes checked. His office is located at 1127 Vermont St My appt was at 1:30 PM I needed to get a pass from Mrs Blanchard, our school secretary She said she thought Dr Warner's office was at 1127 Ohio Ave and not on Vermont St. My mom was right about the address, and I got my eyes checked Now I have another appt with Dr Warner on Thurs, Jan 14, to pick up my glasses. I will tell Mrs Blanchard that Dr Warner's office is on Vermont St and not on Ohio Ave

Last week my mom made an appt. for me at Dr. Warner's office; he is an eye doctor. I had to get my eyes checked. His office is located at 1127 Vermont St. My appt. was at 1:30 P.M. I needed to get a pass from Mrs. Blanchard, our school secretary. She said she thought Dr. Warner's office was at 1127 Ohio Ave. and not on Vermont St. My mom was right about the address, and I got my eyes checked. Now I have another appt. with Dr. Warner on Thurs., Jan. 14, to pick up my glasses. I will tell Mrs. Blanchard that Dr. Warner's office is on Vermont St. and not on Ohio Ave.

© Mark Twain Media, Inc., Publishers 10

Proofreading Punctuation—End Marks: *Exercise 3*

Name: ______________________ Date: ____________

Punctuation—End Marks: *Exercise 3*

Directions: Proofread the following sentences carefully. Use the insert mark to insert the correct word, punctuation, exclamation point, or question mark.

1. I think the ball fell off the table and on to the floor.
2. Where would you like to go on vacation this summer?
3. Wow! look at the beautiful sunset tonight!
4. If you could have three wishes, what would they be?
5. Stop the car!
6. Check the first two or three words on the spelling list.
7. Can you draw a map of the original thirteen colonies?
8. Oh! That bursting balloon startled me.
9. What advice would you give a new student to our school about the lunchroom?
10. Mr. Meyer likes to tell jokes to the class to get them to laugh.
11. I think we lost three of the pieces to this jigsaw puzzle.
12. How long have you been waiting in line to buy a ticket?
13. Hey! Why did you throw that water balloon at me?
14. I think Mike's dog, Rover, is trying to dig a hole under the fence.
15. It's my turn to wash the dishes and your turn to dry them.

© Mark Twain Media, Inc., Publishers 11

Proofreading Punctuation—Apostrophes: *Exercise 1*

Name: ______________________ Date: ____________

Punctuation—Apostrophes: *Exercise 1*

Directions: Rewrite the following paragraph on the lines below, using apostrophes in the correct places.

Im going to the zoo on Friday with my friends. We will ride in my sisters car. My brother isnt going with us. Hed rather do something with his friend Brock. Well get to see Sarahs father because he works at the zoo. He said that we could see the animals up close because hed take us around the cages. I hope to see my favorite animal. It isnt the lion, and it isnt a giraffe; my favorite animal is the elephant. Well walk to the bird house and watch the birds. Maybe some of the birds feathers will be on the ground and well be able to take one. Going to the zoo is great. I dont know of anywhere thats more fun.

I'm going to the zoo on Friday with my friends. We will ride in my sister's car. My brother isn't going with us. He'd rather do something with his friend Brock. We'll get to see Sarah's father because he works at the zoo. He said that we could see the animals up close because he'd take us around the cages. I hope to see my favorite animal. It isn't the lion, and it isn't a giraffe; my favorite animal is the elephant. We'll walk to the bird house and watch the birds. Maybe some of the birds' feathers will be on the ground and we'll be able to take one. Going to the zoo is great. I don't know of anywhere that's more fun.

© Mark Twain Media, Inc., Publishers 13

Proofreading Punctuation—Apostrophes/Quotation Marks: *Exercise 2*

Name: ______________________ Date: ____________

Punctuation—Apostrophes/Quotation Marks: *Exercise 2*

Directions: Proofread the following sentences carefully. Use the correct symbol to insert an apostrophe or quotation marks where needed.

1. Ling said, "Please open the door and help carry in the groceries."
2. I think it's a good book to read and discuss.
3. Carol's sweater is in the lost and found in Mrs. Underwood's room.
4. "Mike," asked Dad, "did you eat the last piece of cherry pie?"
5. "Did you feed the cat its dinner tonight?" asked Dad.
6. Pancho's going to see if he can meet us at the park tomorrow.
7. "Angela, did you get Beth's homework?" asked Mom.
8. I think it's Barb's or Debbie's turn to wash the dishes tonight.
9. Karen can't see the chalkboard without her glasses.
10. "Open your books, but don't begin reading until I tell you to," said Mr. Garcia.
11. I'll need to do my homework early tonight, so I can watch TV.
12. "Todd, do you think you've eaten enough of the cookies?" Carri complained.
13. Let's see how many free throws we can make in five minutes.
14. "Annie," Mrs. Current called, "do you have your mittens, or do you have Mike's?"
15. Look, we'll bring the cake for the party if you can bring the soda.

© Mark Twain Media, Inc., Publishers 14

Answer Keys

Proofreading — Run-on Sentences: *Exercise 1*

Name: ______ Date: ______

Run-on Sentences: *Exercise 1*

Directions: Proofread the following sentences carefully. Correct the run-on sentences, using commas, periods, or semicolons.

1. There are eleven girls in our class there are fourteen boys in our class.
   class, and — class. There
2. Make sure you have your umbrella take your raincoat too.
   umbrella, and — umbrella. Take
3. Jacob is an honor student he always has excellent grades.
   student, and — student. He
4. William had to stay after school he had been talking during math class.
   school, because — school. He
5. Benjamin needed to go to soccer practice he couldn't play in the game if he missed.
   practice, because — practice. He
6. The railroad built a track through town it brought many new businesses to the area.
   town, and — town. It
7. Our family is going to the beach for our vacation my brother will have to miss out.
   vacation, but — vacation. My
8. Come over to my house after school I have the information for our project.
   school, because — school. I
9. I think all I do is write run-on sentences I need to practice my punctuation skills.
   sentences, so — sentences. I
10. When you are giving a speech it is important to speak in a clear voice don't mumble.
    voice, so — voice. Don't

© Mark Twain Media, Inc., Publishers 16

Proofreading — Run-on Sentences: *Exercise 2*

Name: ______ Date: ______

Run-on Sentences: Exercise 2

Directions: Use proofreading marks to mark the corrections that need to be made in the following paragraphs.

Have you ever been to the circus? I remember the first time I went with my mom and dad we had a great time. It was two hours long but the time went by in what seemed like just a few minutes.

When we first walked in after buying our tickets we were greeted by clowns. They had on every color in the rainbow and they all had different makeup on their faces. There were happy clowns and there were sad clowns there were even clowns who looked like they had tears running down their faces.

We found our seats, bought some cotton candy and the show began. There were women and men who flew back and forth on the trapeze. It was amazing to watch them let go and then be caught on the other side. There were animal acts with lions and elephants, tigers and dogs, and horses and ponies. Some people walked on a high wire didn't slip or fall.

The whole day was wonderful I want to go the next time the circus is in town it is the best show to watch.

© Mark Twain Media, Inc., Publishers 17

Proofreading — Combining Sentences: *Exercise 1*

Name: ______ Date: ______

Combining Sentences: *Exercise 1*

Directions: Proofread the following sentences carefully. Combine the sentences on the lines below.

1. John is on the football team. He is president of our class.
   Answers will vary. Teacher check.
2. I want to go to the movies. I also need to clean my room.
3. Jason caught the ball. He almost ran into the fence.
4. Stephen won the school spelling bee. He couldn't go to the state competition.
5. Did you ask Lauren to come to the party? Are you going to wait until later to ask her?
6. Let's have soup for dinner. I will make biscuits.
7. We're watching videos. Mom is making popcorn.
8. I could play tennis after school. I could do my homework.
9. Who brought in the packages? Where did you put my new shirt?
10. Nick will feed the dog. He won't have time to take her for a walk.

© Mark Twain Media, Inc., Publishers 18

Proofreading — Combining Sentences: *Exercise 2*

Name: ______ Date: ______

Combining Sentences: *Exercise 2*

Directions: Rewrite the following paragraph carefully on the lines below, combining sentences as needed.

Last night it snowed. We had to shovel the driveway this morning. It was a difficult job. My older brother Steve helped with it. It took almost all morning. There were three of us shoveling so it went faster. We could have used just shovels. Mr. Adams came with his snow blower.

We came inside. Mom gave us hot chocolate. She put marshmallows in it. We had to hang up our clothes to dry. It didn't take too long. Did we want to go outside again? Did we want to stay in and watch TV?

I really like snow days. It's back to school tomorrow. Did I hear the weatherman say there is a chance of snow tomorrow?

Answers will vary. Teacher check.

© Mark Twain Media, Inc., Publishers 19

Answer Keys

Proofreading — Punctuation Review: *Exercise 1*

Name: ______________________ Date: __________

Punctuation Review: *Exercise 1*

Directions: Proofread the following sentences carefully. Use the correct proofreading marks to show where a correction should be made.

1. I wish I didnt need to get a shot at dr. Davis's office.
2. who is that in the red jacket?
3. Isnt that the worst book you have ever read?
4. My dog out the door this morning and jumped over the fence. (ran)
5. I never grew plants before. This year I planted petunias.
6. "Yes Mr. White replied, there are seven layers of rock in the aquarium."
7. I eat my lunch at 1040 A.M.
8. Allison Jordan and Taylor are all meating me on thrusday afternoon.
9. I think we need too sheats of paper for the test on monday.
10. Me and Jeff were the only ones brave enough to sled down the hill. (I)
11. Whose got the key to the backdoor? (Who's)
12. Mr. Meyer the door before class began. (closed)
13. Have you ever read *harry potter and the chamber of secrets?*
14. I have live in Le Sueur Minnesota and Waukesha Wisconsin.
15. Which jaars may I use for my Science project?

© Mark Twain Media, Inc., Publishers 20

Proofreading — Punctuation Review: *Exercise 2*

Name: ______________________ Date: __________

Punctuation Review: *Exercise 2*

Directions: Proofread the following sentences carefully. Use the correct proofreading marks to show where a correction should be made.

1. I am going to see mrs. Ling before schoool tomorrow.
2. do you know how long the appontment will be?
3. Its going to rain tomorrw when we have our picnic.
4. Where did you find the answer to question number sesven
5. My cat all of the cat food for dinner (ate)
6. Are you going too the movies on saturday
7. I need to rite down your adresss so I can pick you up.
8. If I get the next two two ansers correct I will win the spelling bee.
9. how long do we have too finish the homework assignment?
10. I think I will put the answers on a seperate piece of paper.
11. Carol, Beth, and me are going to decorate the gym for the dance. (I)
12. Mrs. Humphrey said, Make sure that all the clay is put away after the art project."
13. This is the forth day of th week.
14. Zack Juan and Sven have no sisters.
15. Do you think me and Miguel will make the baseball team? (I)

© Mark Twain Media, Inc., Publishers 21

Proofreading — Punctuation Review: *Exercise 3*

Name: ______________________ Date: __________

Punctuation Review: *Exercise 3*

Directions: Proofread the following sentences carefully. Use the correct symbol to insert a colon, a comma, or a semicolon.

1. Are you going to the store or are you going to stay home and watch TV?
2. My mom told me to go to the store and buy the following items a head of lettuce, a quart of milk, a loaf of bread and a stick of butter.
3. Who left their coat hat and sweater on the playground?
4. Have you ever been skiing or do you like to stay inside?
5. My brother lives in Oxford Mississippi.
6. After the morning news I go outside and wait for the bus.
7. My best friend is my dog he goes everywhere with me.
8. For school we need these supplies a three-ring binder, loose-leaf paper, a pencil and a red pen.
9. Mr. Evans the custodian helped us decorate the gym for the dance.
10. I have a large orange cat his name is Tigger.
11. Please help me with my homework then we can play on the computer.
12. I would like to have spaghetti salad garlic bread and pudding for dinner tonight.
13. We invited Mrs. Richter, Mr. Olsen, Mrs. Anderson and Miss Larson to the play.
14. I write great poems but I am not very good at writing paragraphs.
15. Look out the books on that table over there.

© Mark Twain Media, Inc., Publishers 22

Proofreading — Personal Pronouns: *Exercise 1*

Name: ______________________ Date: __________

Personal Pronouns: *Exercise 1*

Directions: Proofread the following sentences carefully. Write "correct" in the blank next to the sentence if it is correct. Write the correct pronoun if it is incorrect.

1. Rodrigo carried the heavy boxes for she. her
2. Them will be here soon to go to the party. They
3. Candice said the fault was hers. Correct
4. You can bring it into the room now. Correct
5. Our is not the car we should be using. Ours
6. Ralph and me are going to the movies on Saturday. I
7. The librarian told them to be quiet in the library. Correct
8. I don't think it was she. Correct
9. Do you think this song would be good for Ann and I to sing? me
10. Samantha and him are taking the notes for the whole class. he
11. Its about time the leak in the ceiling was fixed. It's
12. I don't think your the winner of the election. You're
13. Did you ask them what they're doing after school? Correct
14. Will Sophie give they the candy? them
15. Beth and her will decorate for the school dance. She

© Mark Twain Media, Inc., Publishers 24

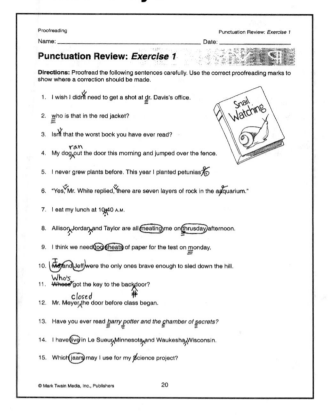

Answer Keys

Proofreading Personal Pronouns: *Exercise 2*

Name: ____________________ Date: __________

Personal Pronouns: *Exercise 2*

Directions: Proofread and correct the following paragraph using proofreading marks.

At our school the sixth grade class has the opportunity to travel to Washington, D.C., in the summer. Last year my class and ~~me~~ I went. ~~Us~~ We sixth graders visited the White House, the Smithsonian Institute, the Capitol, and the Vietnam Memorial. ~~Them~~ They were all great sites. We rode on a plane to Washington, and my best friend Sarah and I got to sit together. ~~Her~~ She and I had a bunch of fun.

~~Us~~ We got to meet several senators at the Capitol. Mr. Richards was ours. We walked around and looked at the different offices. ~~Him~~ He and our other senator have offices next to each other. Next we went to the White House. ~~Their~~ There were guards in every room, but they were helpful and answered all the questions ~~us~~ we had. Sarah and ~~me~~ I walked around and tried to imagine what it was like to live ~~they're~~ there.

The last place we went was the Vietnam Memorial. The big black wall was very impressive. Some people used paper and chalk to make rubbings of the names of ~~there~~ their relatives. These relatives of theirs had died in the war. I don't know whose idea it was to build ~~her~~ it, but it was a good idea.

If ~~your~~ you're ever going to go on a school trip, I hope you go to Washington, D.C. It was great.

© Mark Twain Media, Inc., Publishers 25

Proofreading Pronoun Antecedents: *Exercise 1*

Name: ____________________ Date: __________

Pronoun Antecedents: *Exercise 1*

Directions: Read the following sentences carefully. Circle the correct pronoun for its antecedent.

1. Neither of the boys was happy when (**his**, their) dad told him he had to do chores.
2. Mike went to the grocery store; (**he**, she) bought bread and milk.
3. Wilma bought a new tennis racket. (**Hers**, Theirs, Its) was an expensive brand.
4. Ben and Sue played a new ball game; (**it**, they) was a lot of fun.
5. We had spaghetti for dinner; (she, **it**) was delicious.
6. Many hoped this would be the winning point. It was a disappointment to (they, **them**).
7. The elephant knelt down; (**it**, he) was still twice as tall as the trainer.
8. One of the dogs did tricks on command. (They, **It**) was a smart dog.
9. Erica gave everybody presents. (He, **We**) were happy to get (**them**, it).
10. How did people know (he, **it**, they) when the parade started?
11. One girl asked if (**she**, it, they) could answer the question.
12. She put her money in the bank. I don't know what to do with (it, **mine**, hers).
13. I put the books away. Did you wonder where (**they**, them) were?
14. Several of the cats were eating dinner. (**They**, It) each had a bowl.
15. Each man had a plan. Each thought (hers, **his**, its) was the best.

© Mark Twain Media, Inc., Publishers 27

Proofreading Pronoun Antecedents: *Exercise 2*

Name: ____________________ Date: __________

Pronoun Antecedents: *Exercise 2*

Directions: Rewrite the following paragraphs on the lines below. Correct any pronoun antecedent errors.

If you are going to have a pet, you need to know beforehand how to take care of it. Pets require a lot of time and effort if it is to live a healthy life. There are several things you must know in order to take care of any pet.

First you need to find a place for your pet to live. A dog will need a bed to sleep in and a place that they can go to get away from everyone if it wants. A cat will sleep wherever they want to. If you have a bird, you need to get a cage for them and make sure it is not in a drafty place.

Dogs, cats, and birds all need places for it to eat. A bird will eat in its cage unless you train it to eat somewhere else. Dogs and cats like to eat their meals somewhere where there isn't a lot of people who might bump into them.

All animals like to be exercised. If your pet just lies around the house all day, she will not be healthy, and they will get fat.

Make sure you take good care of your pets, and it will live with you for a long time.

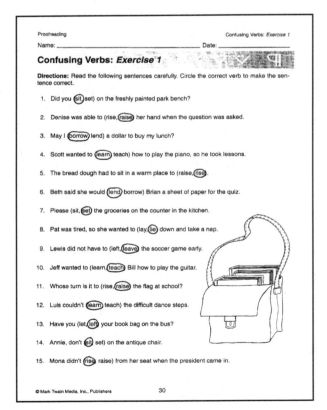

If you are going to have a pet, you need to know beforehand how to take care of it. Pets require a lot of time and effort if they are to live healthy lives. There are several things you must know in order to take care of any pet.

First you need to find a place for your pet to live. A dog will need a bed to sleep in and a place that it can go to get away from everyone if it wants. A cat will sleep wherever it wants to. If you have a bird, you need to get a cage for it and make sure it is not in a drafty place.

Dogs, cats, and birds all need places for them to eat. A bird will eat in its cage unless you train it to eat somewhere else. Dogs and cats like to eat their meals somewhere where there aren't a lot of people who might bump into them.

All animals like to be exercised. If your pet just lies around the house all day, it will not be healthy, and it will get fat.

Make sure you take good care of your pets, and they will live with you for a long time.

© Mark Twain Media, Inc., Publishers 28

Proofreading Confusing Verbs: *Exercise 1*

Name: ____________________ Date: __________

Confusing Verbs: *Exercise 1*

Directions: Read the following sentences carefully. Circle the correct verb to make the sentence correct.

1. Did you (**sit**, set) on the freshly painted park bench?
2. Denise was able to (rise, **raise**) her hand when the question was asked.
3. May I (**borrow**, lend) a dollar to buy my lunch?
4. Scott wanted to (**learn**, teach) how to play the piano, so he took lessons.
5. The bread dough had to sit in a warm place to (raise, **rise**).
6. Beth said she would (**lend**, borrow) Brian a sheet of paper for the quiz.
7. Please (sit, **set**) the groceries on the counter in the kitchen.
8. Pat was tired, so she wanted to (lay, **lie**) down and take a nap.
9. Lewis did not have to (left, **leave**) the soccer game early.
10. Jeff wanted to (learn, **teach**) Bill how to play the guitar.
11. Whose turn is it to (rise, **raise**) the flag at school?
12. Luis couldn't (**learn**, teach) the difficult dance steps.
13. Have you (let, **left**) your book bag on the bus?
14. Annie, don't (**sit**, set) on the antique chair.
15. Mona didn't (**rise**, raise) from her seat when the president came in.

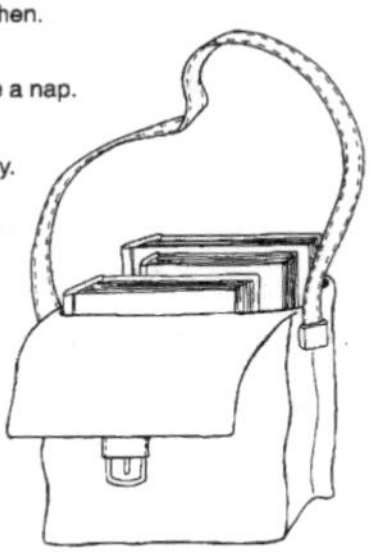

© Mark Twain Media, Inc., Publishers 30

Answer Keys

Proofreading — Confusing Verbs: *Exercise 2*

Name: ______________________ Date: ____________

Confusing Verbs: *Exercise 2*

Directions: Proofread and correct the following paragraph using proofreading marks.

I wanted to ~~learn~~ teach Bill a lesson about money. He always forgets his lunch money. Every day during history he comes up to me.

"Will you ~~borrow~~ lend me seventy-five cents for lunch?" Bill asks.

"Yes, but this is the last time," I reply.

"Oh, yeah, we'll see about that," he answers. [apostrophe inserted]

Then I ~~sit~~ set the money on his desk, he takes it and puts it in his pocket, and he doesn't remember that he borrowed money from me. It is never the last time, though, because I give him the money each time. I am always afraid of what he will do if I say no. This is not helping Bill learn to be more responsible, and it is hurting my savings. [comma inserted]

Now I only take enough money for my lunch at school, or I bring my lunch from home. [comma inserted] The first day I did this, Bill came up to me during history and said, "Will you ~~borrow~~ lend me seventy-five cents for lunch?"

I answered in a very firm voice, "No, I only have enough for my lunch today."

Bill moaned, "You always ~~leave~~ let me borrow money from you."

I stood my ground and said, "No." Then I waited for his reaction.

Bill looked at me; his arm ~~rose~~ raised up. I backed away, but he slapped me on the back anyway and said, "No problem, buddy." Then he ~~set~~ sat back down in his chair.

Guess I learned a lesson too.

© Mark Twain Media, Inc., Publishers 31

Proofreading — Subject-Verb Agreement: *Exercise 1*

Name: ______________________ Date: ____________

Subject-Verb Agreement: *Exercise 1*

Directions: Proofread the following sentences carefully. Write correct in the blank below the sentence if it is correct. Rewrite the sentence if it is incorrect, correcting any errors in subject-verb agreement.

1. Jeff and Susan is going to be the speakers at the assembly.
   Jeff and Susan are going to be the speakers at the assembly.
2. Carmela are going to be the bridesmaid at her brother's wedding.
   Carmela is going to be the bridesmaid at her brother's wedding.
3. Either Miguel or Angela is going to run for class president.
   correct
4. Can you see if Tracey and Maria is coming over to our house?
   Can you see if Tracey and Maria are coming over to our house?
5. Either Brian or Barbara are taking the dog for a walk.
   Either Brian or Barbara is taking the dog for a walk.
6. Who run the tape recorder while we sing?
   Who runs the tape recorder while we sing?
7. There is ten amendments to the Constitution that are called the Bill of Rights.
   There are ten amendments to the Constitution that are called the Bill of Rights.
8. Jay and Elena thinks that it would be a good idea to start a newspaper.
   Jay and Elena think that it would be a good idea to start a newspaper.
9. Neither Sherry nor Lisa will be going to the movies tonight.
   correct
10. Mrs. Graham asked us to turn our papers in when we was finished.
    Mrs. Graham asked us to turn our papers in when we were finished.

© Mark Twain Media, Inc., Publishers 33

Proofreading — Subject-Verb Agreement: *Exercise 2*

Name: ______________________ Date: ____________

Subject-Verb Agreement: *Exercise 2*

Directions: Rewrite the following paragraph on the lines below, correcting any errors in subject-verb agreement.

Next year I hopes to play the flute in the school orchestra. I has been taking lessons from Mrs. Elliot for three years. I think it is time for me to try out for the orchestra. I know I has had excellent lessons, and I have practiced every day. I still worries about standing in front of all the music teachers and playing my flute. It would be so easy to put my fingers in the wrong place or to holds my lip wrong. Neither my mom nor my dad think I will have any trouble at the audition, but I is not as sure. I still has a few months to practice and work at being brave. I hopes I gets to play in the school orchestra.

Next year I hope to play the flute in the school orchestra. I have been taking lessons from Mrs. Elliot for three years. I think it is time for me to try out for the orchestra. I know I have had excellent lessons, and I have practiced every day. I still worry about standing in front of all the music teachers and playing my flute. It would be so easy to put my fingers in the wrong place or to hold my lip wrong. Neither my mom nor my dad thinks I will have any trouble at the audition, but I am not as sure. I still have a few months to practice and work at being brave. I hope I get to play in the school orchestra.

© Mark Twain Media, Inc., Publishers 34

Proofreading — Compound Subjects and Indefinite Pronouns: *Exercise 1*

Name: ______________________ Date: ____________

Compound Subjects and Indefinite Pronouns: *Exercise 1*

Directions: Read the following sentences carefully. Circle the correct verb to make the sentence correct.

1. The baker and his assistants (starts, **start**) work early at the bakery.
2. Can Angie and Nick (**take**, takes) the dog for a walk?
3. Multiplication tables and division (**require**, requires) memorization.
4. Neither a basketball game nor tennis lessons (interests, **interest**) me today.
5. Either Jason or Luis (are, **is**) our starting pitcher tomorrow.
6. Your aunt and uncle (is, **are**) on their vacation in Mexico.
7. Colorful candies and a candle (decorates, **decorate**) the top of the cake.
8. Neither these boys nor that girl (**wants**, want) to walk to school in the cold.
9. The cat and her kittens (**howl**, howls) when they are hungry.
10. Either my brother or my dad (go, **goes**) to the doughnut shop on Saturday mornings.
11. Neither my sisters nor my mom (are, **is**) feeling very well today.
12. Mrs. Harrison's and Mrs. Morgan's classes (**are**, is) at the planetarium.
13. The bookcase shelves (is, **are**) full of books to read.
14. Eric and Beth (**ride**, rides) their bikes to school every day.
15. How many days (is, **are**) Karen and Marion going to be on vacation?

© Mark Twain Media, Inc., Publishers 36

Answer Keys

Proofreading Compound Subjects and Indefinite Pronouns: *Exercise 2*

Name: ______________________ Date: ______________

Compound Subjects and Indefinite Pronouns: *Exercise 2*

Directions: Read the following sentences carefully. Underline the indefinite pronoun, and then circle the correct verb to make the sentence correct.

1. Laura uses pen and ink for her drawings, but others (**use** uses) watercolors.
2. Does anyone (**ride** rides) his or her bike to the park?
3. I hope neither of the kittens (are, **is**) out in the yard.
4. All of the cast of the play (**bow** bows) at the final curtain call.
5. A few of the art students (helps, **help**) paint scenery.
6. Everybody (**wants** want) a day with no homework.
7. Each of you (carry, **carries**) a bag of groceries into the house.
8. Something (**is** are) missing from the puzzle.
9. Mrs. Evans said everyone (are, **is**) going on the field trip.
10. Neither of the girls (**is** are) babysitting on Saturday.
11. Did you say both of the sweaters (is, **are**) Ramona's?
12. One of the puppies (are, **is**) sleeping in my lap.
13. I think someone (**is** are) going to volunteer to give their speech first.
14. All of the students (**cheer** cheers) at the football game.
15. Most of the puppies (**sleep** sleeps) during the day.

© Mark Twain Media, Inc., Publishers 37

Proofreading Compound Subjects and Indefinite Pronouns: *Exercise 3*

Name: ______________________ Date: ______________

Compound Subjects and Indefinite Pronouns: *Exercise 3*

Directions: Rewrite the following paragraph on the lines below, correcting any agreement errors.

Neither Jeff nor Ben are going out for the football team this year. Each of these boys has decided to play soccer instead. All of the soccer team is happy to have them join the team. The team feel that each of the boys has qualities that will help them to a championship season. Jeff has played soccer before when he was in second and third grade, but Ben has never played on a team. Many of the plays the boys will be learning is similar to plays in football. Some of the players is planning to help both boys becomes better acquainted with soccer and the rules.

Neither Jeff nor Ben is going out for football this year. Each of these boys has decided to play soccer instead. All of the soccer team are happy to have them join the team. The team feels that each of the boys has qualities that will help it to a championship season. Jeff has played soccer before when he was in second and third grade, but Ben has never played on a team. Many of the plays the boys will be learning are similar to plays in football. Some of the players are planning to help both boys become better acquainted with soccer and the rules.

© Mark Twain Media, Inc., Publishers 38

Proofreading Subject-Verb Arrangement: *Exercise 1*

Name: ______________________ Date: ______________

Subject-Verb Arrangement: *Exercise 1*

Directions: Proofread the following sentences carefully. Circle the correct verb for its subject to make the sentence correct.

1. Where (**is** are) the book that goes on this shelf?
2. Under the porch (live, **lives**) a family of mice.
3. Here (is, **are**) the lists of overdue library books.
4. To the gym (**go** goes) students who need schedule changes.
5. There (**is** are) no one in the electronics department who can answer my question.
6. At the Mardi Gras celebration (was, **were**) many strange costumes.
7. The captain of the team (**takes** take) the roster to the umpire.
8. (Was, **Were**) they late for school again?
9. There (is, **are**) better examples of evaporation than the one you chose.
10. (Is, **Are**) Jamal and Luisa the only ones going to the meeting?
11. Here (**is** are) the best title for your book.
12. After practice (was heard, **were heard**) many heated arguments about the disputed call.
13. Under the microscope (appears, **appear**) small living creatures.
14. (Is, **Are**) a jonquil and a daffodil the same flower?
15. There (is, **are**) usually more people waiting in line for the movie.

© Mark Twain Media, Inc., Publishers 40

Proofreading Verb Tense: *Exercise 1*

Name: ______________________ Date: ______________

Verb Tense: *Exercise 1*

Directions: Proofread the following sentences carefully. Circle the correct verb tense to make the sentence correct.

1. In 1861, the North and South (starts, **started**) a civil war.
2. By the end of the day, Mike had (**cleaned** cleans) his room.
3. Scott (participate, **had participated**) in every spelling bee.
4. If you eat this one too, you (eats, **will have eaten**) all of my birthday treats.
5. Jonathan (**has picked** pick) enough apples for a pie.
6. Matt (**looked** look) in every classroom for his books.
7. Last night we (make, **made**) decorations for the school dance.
8. Phil (**will practice** practice) his piano piece many times.
9. As a joke, they (wears, **wore**) matching outfits all week.
10. Wendy (**has known** knows) David for a long time.
11. Next month, Annie (was, **will have been**) in charge of the choir for two years.
12. Yesterday, Carol (**wrote** write) a letter to the editor.
13. Our class (**received** receive) a letter from the President of the United States.
14. Mrs. Garcia (help, **helps**) me understand my math.
15. We (tested, **will test**) all of the pens to see if they have ink.

© Mark Twain Media, Inc., Publishers 42

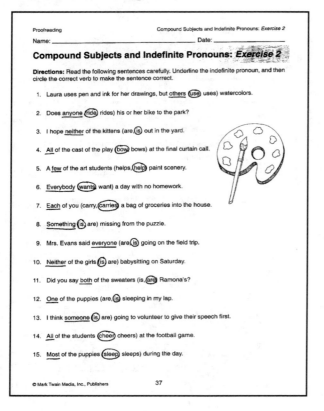

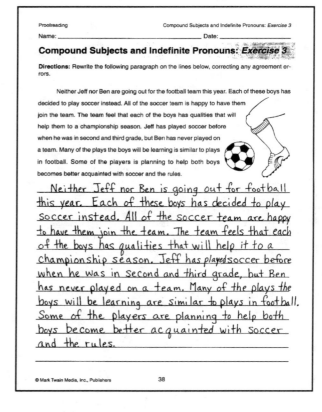

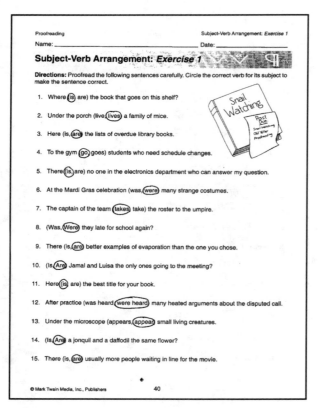

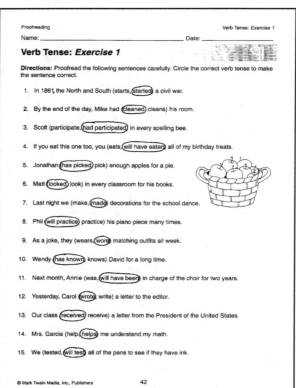

Answer Keys

Proofreading Verb Tense: *Exercise 2*

Name: ______________________ Date: ____________

Verb Tense: *Exercise 2*

Directions: Rewrite the following paragraph on the lines below, correcting any errors in verb tense.

Storms is interesting weather phenomena. First an approaching storm created a large cloud. You can see the cloud in the sky as it got dark. Sometimes, when a storm is approaching, the temperature dropped. The storm gets closer, and the sky gets darker. When there was a storm, it can rain, hail, sleet, or even snow. Some storms caused a tornadoes. Tornadoes cause strong winds. The winds lasted for a few moments, but it can seem like hours. Storms have thunder and lightning. Even some tornadoes did have thunder and lightning. Storms were a powerful weather system.

Storms are interesting weather phenomena. First an approaching storm creates a large cloud. You can see the cloud in the sky as it gets dark. Sometimes, when a storm is approaching, the temperature drops. The storm gets closer, and the sky gets darker. When there is a storm, it can rain, hail, sleet, or even snow. Some storms cause tornadoes. Tornadoes cause strong winds. The winds last for a few moments, but it can seem like hours. Storms have thunder and lightning. Even some tornadoes have thunder and lightning. Storms are powerful weather systems.

© Mark Twain Media, Inc., Publishers 43

Proofreading Comparisons: *Introduction*

Name: ______________________ Date: ____________

Comparisons: *Exercise 1*

Directions: Proofread the following sentences carefully. Write correct on the line below the sentence if it is correct. Rewrite the sentence if it is incorrect, correcting any errors in comparisons.

1. After school, I am having a sandwich and the most largest soda I can find.
   After school, I am having a sandwich and the largest soda I can find.
2. I think the sense of smell is the stronger sense in animals.
   I think the sense of smell is the strongest sense in animals.
3. Mrs. Ripley said that I had the goodest grade on the test of anyone in the class.
   Mrs. Ripley said that I had the best grade on the test of anyone in the class.
4. Mr. Nelson was the bravest person in the room when the snake slithered in.
   correct
5. Which baby is cuter, the one dressed in yellow or the one dressed in green?
   correct
6. Which of the three teachers gets to school the most early?
   Which of the three teachers gets to school the earliest?
7. Even when the storm was at its baddest, our electrical power didn't go out.
   Even when the storm was at its worst, our electrical power didn't go out.
8. One of the two plays is more popular than the other.
   correct
9. I think life in the 1950s was a simpler time than life today.
   correct
10. Taming wild animals must be the more dangerous job of any I have heard of.
    Taming wild animals must be the most dangerous job of any I have heard of.

© Mark Twain Media, Inc., Publishers 45

Proofreading Comparisons: *Exercise 2*

Name: ______________________ Date: ____________

Comparisons: *Exercise 2*

Directions: Rewrite the following paragraph on the lines below, correcting any errors in usage.

The sadder book I have ever read is *Old Yeller* by Fred Gipson. It is the story of a boy and his dog. There are many animal books that are interesting, and some are sad, but this is the goodest one I have read. Old Yeller comes to the cattle ranch and is adopted by Travis. They become the bestest of friends. They do everything together, and the dog watches over the family and the ranch. The love between the boy and his dog is the realest. The words on the pages made me think of my own dog and how I love it. There are parts in the book that you feel as if you are actually there with them. It is a sad book, and I cried more hard at the end.

The saddest book I have ever read is Old Yeller by Fred Gipson. It is the story of a boy and his dog. There are many animal books that are interesting, and some are sad, but this is the best one I have read. Old Yeller comes to the cattle ranch and is adopted by Travis. They become the best of friends. They do everything together, and the dog watches over the family and the ranch. The love between the boy and his dog is real. The words on the pages made me think of my own dog and how I love it. There are parts in the book that you feel as if you are actually there with them. It is a sad book, and I cried hardest at the end.

© Mark Twain Media, Inc., Publishers 46

Proofreading Modifiers: *Exercise 1*

Name: ______________________ Date: ____________

Modifiers: *Exercise 1*

Directions: Proofread the following sentences carefully. Circle the correct modifier to make the sentence correct. Underline the word the modifier modifies.

1. Our sailboats drifted (quiet, quietly) across the pond.
2. You appear (happy, happily) on this early morning.
3. Our music group sang (bad, badly) today during rehearsal.
4. Maggie yelled (loud, loudly) at her brother.
5. If we walk (real, really) quickly, we can get home before my brother.
6. Our book club meets (regular, regularly) even during the summer.
7. Did you open the door (cautious, cautiously)?
8. Apples and oranges are a (good, well) source of vitamins.
9. I (happy, happily) ate the last piece of chocolate cake.
10. Carrie was (complete, completely) honest when she talked with the teacher.
11. Last night the band played really (good, well) during the performance.
12. Do you think this music is too (slow, slowly) for the start of the pep rally?
13. The artist used (beautiful, beautifully) colors to paint the picture.
14. Do you think that extreme sports will be (real, really) popular?
15. Amanda read the poem (beautiful, beautifully) to the audience.

© Mark Twain Media, Inc., Publishers 48

Answer Keys

Proofreading — Modifiers: *Exercise 2*

Name: ______________________ Date: ______________

Modifiers: *Exercise 2*

Directions: Rewrite the following paragraph on the lines below, correcting any errors in the use of modifiers.

Students who practice their musical instruments do good in their recitals. If you don't practice, you will play bad. The people sitting at the recital will think the time is passing real slowly if they have to listen to students who don't know the right notes to play. You can tell the students who are confidently. They come on the stage and sit careful on the edge of the chair and wait for the conductor to give them a signal. A student who is not prepared fumbles through his or her music and tries not to make eye contact with the conductor. It is much better to practice, so when you have a recital, you will feel confident, and the audience will enjoy your performance.

Students who practice their musical instruments do well in their recitals. If you don't practice, you will play badly. The people sitting at the recital will think the time is passing really slowly if they have to listen to students who don't know the right notes to play. You can tell the students who are confident. They come on stage and sit carefully on the edge of the chair and wait for the conductor to give them a signal. A student who is not prepared fumbles through his or her music and tries not to make eye contact with the conductor. It is much better to practice, so when you have a recital, you will feel confident, and the audience will enjoy your performance.

© Mark Twain Media, Inc., Publishers 49

Proofreading — Double Negatives: *Exercise 1*

Name: ______________________ Date: ______________

Double Negatives: *Exercise 1*

Directions: Proofread the following sentences carefully. Write correct on the line below the sentence if it is correct. Rewrite the sentence if it is incorrect, correcting any double negatives.

1. There wasn't hardly enough food in the box to feed the dog.
   was hardly enough — wasn't enough
2. We don't want no extra people on the decoration committee.
   We want no — We don't want any
3. Do you want anything from the grocery store?
   Correct
4. None of them had nothing to help fix up the playground equipment.
   None of them had anything — They had nothing
5. There wasn't no money left to pay for the food for the party.
   There was no money — There wasn't any money
6. The splinter was so small, you could hardly see it.
   correct
7. The information Karen and Suzy found for their report wasn't no good.
   wasn't any good — was no good
8. Have you ever eaten chocolate-covered grasshoppers?
   Correct
9. Weren't none of the hockey players on the ice when you got to the arena?
   Weren't any of — Were none of
10. I have never learned how to paint with watercolors.
    Correct

© Mark Twain Media, Inc., Publishers 50

Proofreading — Double Negatives: *Exercise 2*

Name: ______________________ Date: ______________

Double Negatives: *Exercise 2*

Directions: Rewrite the following paragraph on the lines below, correcting any errors in the use of double negatives.

There hasn't hardly been a week at school better than last week. We didn't have no tests in any of our classes. There really wasn't scarcely any homework either. We had two assemblies during the week, too. One was a musical production, and one was a pep rally for our basketball team. During the one for the musical production, we didn't do nothing except sit and listen to the singing and dancing. They really did a nice job. Afterwards, the music teacher told us we should think about joining the choir when we go to high school. I don't think she meant me, because I don't have no talent. During the assembly for the basketball team, we did cheers and yells and listened to how good they had played during the year. I really like weeks when we don't have nothing to do.

There has hardly been a week at school better than last week. We didn't have any tests in any of our classes. There really wasn't any homework either. We had two assemblies during the week, too. One was a musical production, and one was a pep rally for our basketball team. During the one for the musical production, we didn't do anything except sit and listen to the singing and dancing. They really did a nice job. Afterwards, the music teacher told us we should think about joining the choir when we go to high school. I don't think she meant me, because I have no talent. During the assembly for the basketball team, we did cheers and yells and listened to how well they had played during the year. I really like weeks when we don't have anything to do.

© Mark Twain Media, Inc., Publishers 51

Proofreading — Capitalization: *Exercise 1*

Name: ______________________ Date: ______________

Capitalization: *Exercise 1*

Directions: Proofread the following sentences carefully. Mark the letters that need to be capitalized with the correct proofreading symbol.

1. I live at 2214 maine st.
2. Do you think mrs. brown and mrs. everly will chaperone the party?
3. athens is the capital of what country?
4. The title of the book is *how to maintain and repair bicycles.*
5. The weatherman said that there would be twelve inches of snow in buffalo, new york.
6. Ben told the class that president bush was living in the white house.
7. I am supposed to meet melissa at the corner of oak and spring streets.
8. Was thomas jefferson the third president?
9. Do jim and shelly have practice on monday or tuesday?
10. my dog rusty sleeps in the laundry room.
11. Sonja and lester are going to a world series game in chicago.
12. Mr. nelson teaches math, history, and english at our school.
13. I would like to visit london, england, and rome, italy.
14. John Adams and Benjamin Franklin worked on the declaration of independence.
15. Steven is going to the strike and spare bowling alley after school today.

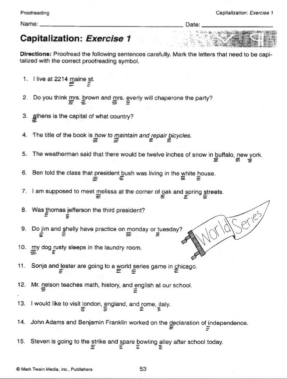

© Mark Twain Media, Inc., Publishers 53

Answer Keys

Proofreading | Capitalization: *Exercise 2*

Name: ______________________ Date: ____________

Capitalization: *Exercise 2*

Directions: Proofread the following paragraph carefully. Use the correct symbols to show letters that should be capitalized or letters that should be lower case.

My aunt and I went to the art museum to see the exhibit of monet paintings. I was supposed to go on a field trip with my Art class to the Museum, but I was sick that day and missed it. aunt barbara said that she would take me when I was well. We rode the train from the suburbs to downtown chicago. It was great to look out the window and see all the scenery flying by. The Train Station was just like it looks on TV with people rushing by on their way to work. At the Museum there was so much to see. We looked at several other exhibits before we went in to the monet area, where the paintings were hung on the walls. There were benches where you could sit and study the paintings. Some of the artists' paintings looked like my younger Sister had painted them. Others were so beautiful, I didn't want to leave. But the monet exhibit was the best of all; I thought I could stay in that room forever. I whispered to aunt Barbara, "don't you wish you could paint like that? I know i do." On the train ride home, I looked out the window and saw the scenery the way monet must have looked at it, not just flying by, but in blues and greens and yellows. I always thought History was my favorite subject, but now I think it's Art.

© Mark Twain Media, Inc., Publishers 54

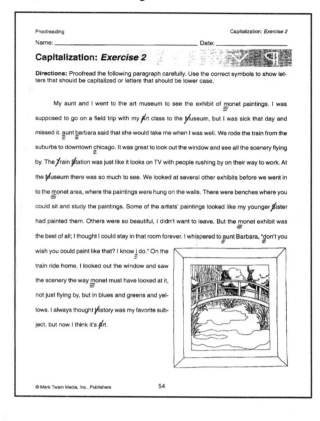

Proofreading | Colloquialisms: *Exercise 1*

Name: ______________________ Date: ____________

Colloquialisms: *Exercise 1*

Directions: Proofread the following sentences carefully. Rewrite the sentences on the lines below, using formal English.

1. I saw the neatest outfit on sale at the mall yesterday.
   Answers will vary.
2. Old man Morris always gives me the creeps.
3. Jonathan was just like all the other little rug rats.
4. I shouldn'ta been out later than my curfew.
5. I gotta get home before dinner tonight.
6. I received ten bucks for cleaning the yard; I am in the money now.
7. Do you think that school oughta start an hour later?
8. Winter is always cold and icky.
9. George Washington was an awesome president.
10. Where did you find that way cool bicycle?

© Mark Twain Media, Inc., Publishers 56

Proofreading | Colloquialisms: *Exercise 2*

Name: ______________________ Date: ____________

Colloquialisms: *Exercise 2*

Directions: Rewrite the following paragraph on the lines below, correcting any errors in the use of colloquialisms.

Wow! I saw the coolest thing today. My buddy and I were out, just hanging around, when a fire truck went screaming by us. We thought that was awesome, so we hopped on our bikes and went high-tailing after it. That truck could really move; it was hard to keep up with it. I bet we followed that buggy for at least eight blocks. The firemen were hanging on the back of the truck, and it looked like a couple more guys were riding inside, plus there was the driver and the guy in the passenger's seat. Jason, my pal, wanted to stop after a couple of blocks, but I said no way, we weren't going to let this one get away. I peddled my bike with all my heart. Finally, the firetruck turned a corner, and we heard it stop. By the time we got around the corner, the truck had just pulled into the station. I thought it was going to go somewhere neat, like a huge fire, but it had just been out on a practice run. I wasn't blue though, because the firemen let us look at the truck while they put things away. No problem, we still thought it was far out.

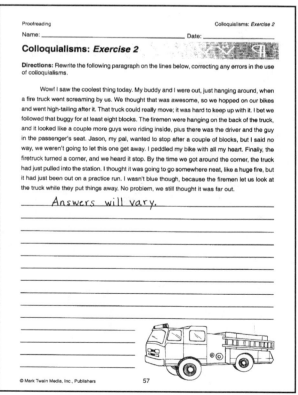

Answers will vary.

© Mark Twain Media, Inc., Publishers 57

Proofreading | Proofreading Review: *Exercise 1*

Name: ______________________ Date: ____________

Proofreading Review: *Exercise 1*

Directions: Proofread the following paragraph for misspelled or misused words. Circle each misspelled or misused word, and write the correct word on one of the lines below.

My favoritest place to visit is the zoo in our town. It is located not to far from my house, so I can walk there whenever I chose. Today, I started my visit at the lion house. While I was their, I watched the great yellow cats prowl around they're outside enclosure. Next, I visited the monkeys, who entertained me by running around and climbing trees. Then I choose to stop and feed the ducks some peaces of bred that I had brought along. I sat very quiet, and soon a mother duck and her ducklings came up and ate from my hand. I finished my visit by going to the seal pond. Its fun to watch them sun themselves on the rocks or swim in their deep, green pond. After a while, I looked at my watch and realized it was time to go home. Today at the zoo was the best day yet!

1. favorite	2. too
3. Choose	4. there
5. their	6. chose
7. pieces	8. bread
9. quietly	10. It's

© Mark Twain Media, Inc., Publishers 58

Answer Keys

Name: ______________________ Date: ____________

Proofreading Review: *Exercise 2*

Directions: Proofread the following paragraph for misspelled or misused words. Circle each misspelled or misused word, and write the correct word on one of the lines below.

After our school trip to the bank, I think that being a bank teller is the most funnest and exciting job. A bank teller does many different things in the bank. He or she handles transactions for customers, such as deposits and withdrawls. A teller also takes cutomers loan payments and helps them fix any problems they have in there accounts.

Some bank tellers also work in the drive-through to help customers who do not want to get out of their cars. Being in the drive-through is a more fast-paced area then working in the lobby. They're can be many different lanes of cars, and the teller has to be sure to keep them all straight.

Working in a bank can also be very interesting, because it allows you to meat and talk to different people every day. The other people who work at the bank are also very nice. They took us on a tour of the vault and let many of the students use the coin counter to add up there change.

Our trip to the bank was very unformative and I think that I wood like to work at a bank.

1. fun
2. withdrawals
3. Customers'
4. their
5. than
6. There
7. meet
8. their
9. informative
10. would

Name: ______________________ Date: ____________

Proofreading Review: *Exercise 3*

Directions: Proofread the following paragraph for misspelled or misused words. Circle each misspelled or misused word, and write the correct word on one of the lines below.

One day, my dad and I decided to plant a garden in are backyard. My dad has done a lot of gardening, and he said he would learn me. We began by bying packages of seeds from a gardening store down the street from our house. We picked out carrots, lettuce, daisies, and marigolds. After changing into old close, we dug up a section of dirt in the backyard. Then I poked holes in the soft, brown dirt and dropped one seed into each whole. When all the seeds had been planted, I covered them up with dirt and watered them well with the hose. I make labels for each of the different plants to show were each type of seed had been planted. Every day, I check on the garden to make sure there are know weeds growing and that the plants are being watered. In a few weaks, we will have fresh vegetables to eat and flowers to share with our friends. Its very easy to start a garden.

1. our
2. teach
3. buying
4. clothes
5. hole
6. made
7. where
8. no
9. weeks
10. It's

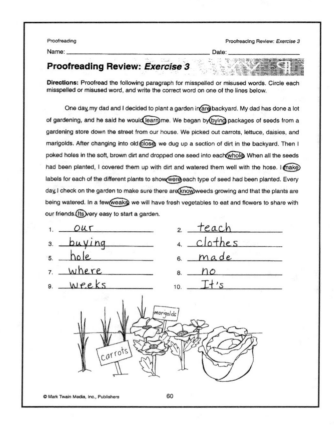

Name: ______________________ Date: ____________

Proofreading Review: *Exercise 4*

Directions: Proofread the following paragraph for misspelled or misused words. Circle each misspelled or misused word, and write the correct word on one of the lines below.

There are several things you should do to study for a test. The first things you need are a positive atitude and a quite place to do you're studying. You may think its nice to study with the radio or TV on, but you are really not giving the subject your studying enough attention. The next thing to do is to review each chapter that will be covered by the test to see what important things or stressed in that chapter. It is also helpful to read over any notes from the chapters, highlighting important words, names, and dates. Next, try looking at just the highlighted words and quiz yourself. Be sure to look up any knew vocabulary words that you are unsure of or that your teacher said were important. It is also essential to go to the end of each chapter to answer any review questions. Write down the answers; then look at the answers to see if you can tell what the question is. When you feel you can answer the questions without having to look up the answers or refer to your notes, you are already to take the test. If you study careful before a test, you are on your way to recieving a good grade!

1. attitude
2. quiet
3. your
4. it's
5. you're
6. are
7. new
8. all ready
9. Carefully
10. receiving

Name: ______________________ Date: ____________

Proofreading Review: *Exercise 5*

Directions: Proofread the following paragraph for misspelled or misused words. Circle each misspelled or misused word, and write the correct word on one of the lines below.

This summer my friends and I went to a Renaissance Fare held in are town. It was very exciting. It was held in a large open field, and all around it were sit up little booths and tents. Many of the people who were visiting were dressed in medieval clothing. The woman wore long dresses and pointy hats with veils on their heads. Many of the men wore tights and carryed swords. I looked at all the booths that were selling things first. There was one that sold handmade jewlery and another that sold dryed floral wreaths for people to wear on their heads. I stopped at a booth celling food and bought a giant turkey leg to eat for lunch. In the afternoon there was a jousting tournament to watch. Knights on horses charged down the field and tried to knock each other off there horses. There was also a demonstration of sword fighting. We really enjoyed our visit too the Renaissance Fair.

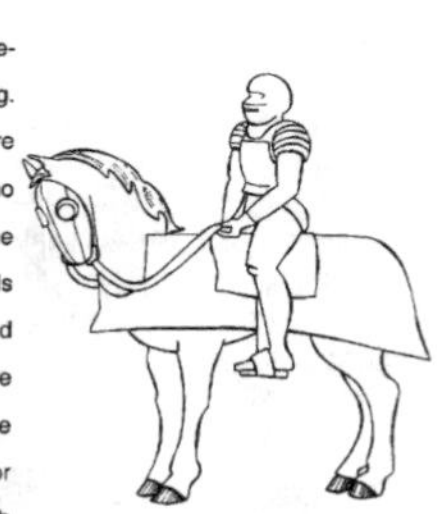

1. Fair
2. our
3. set
4. women
5. Carried
6. jewelry
7. dried
8. selling
9. their
10. to

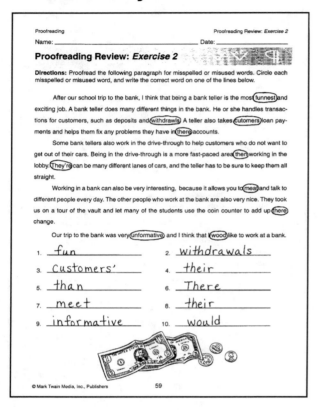

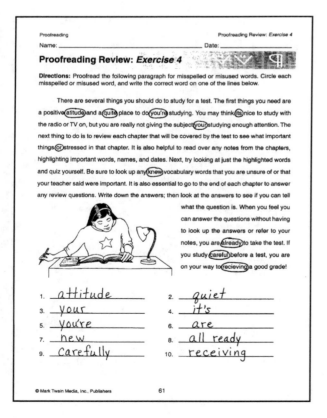

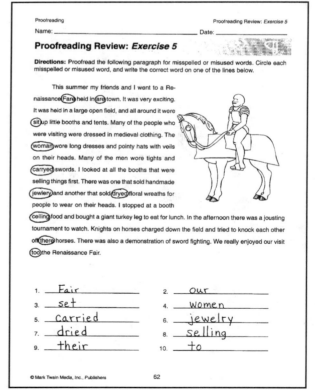

Answer Keys

Proofreading — Proofreading Review: *Exercise 6*

Name: ______________________ Date: ______________

Proofreading Review: *Exercise 6*

Directions: Proofread the following paragraph for capitalization errors. Circle each error, and write the correct word on one of the lines below.

This summer my Mom and Dad took my brother and me to London, england. One of the most exciting things I got to do for the first time was to ride in an airplane. We had to arrive at the Airport a few hours early, so we could check in our bags and have our tickets stamped. The airport was very large, and we had to walk a long way to get to the plane. I was surprised at how small the plane was inside. Everyone had to sit very close together; there was not much room to stretch our legs. Then the plane started rushing down the runway, and suddenly we were in the air. The flight was very long, but we tried to keep busy to make the time pass more quickly. Mom and dad watched a movie for part of the flight. My Brother and I played cards. We also were able to sleep for a while with pillows that were provided by the Airline. Then the Flight Attendant served us dinner on little plastic trays. The landing was very exciting as well. As we got closer to london, we could look out the window and see all sorts of little towns and buildings. I really enjoyed my first plane trip.

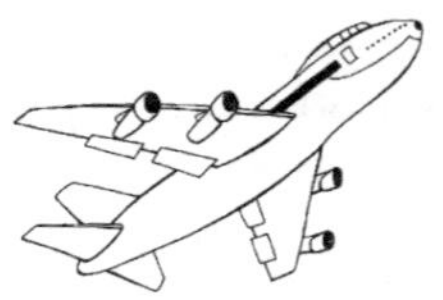

1. mom	2. dad
3. England	4. airport
5. Dad	6. brother
7. airline	8. flight
9. attendant	10. London

© Mark Twain Media, Inc., Publishers 63

Proofreading — Proofreading Review: *Exercise 7*

Name: ______________________ Date: ______________

Proofreading Review: *Exercise 7*

Directions: Proofread the following paragraph for capitalization errors. Circle each error, and write the correct word on one of the lines below.

Today we got a new dog. We have never had a dog before, only cats. My Mom and dad told my Sister and me to do some research, so we could decide which kind of dog we would like to get. First, we went to the Pet Store to look at the different types of dogs. We also read many books about different breeds to see what type of dog would be best for our family. We didn't want one that was too loud and barked too much, but we didn't want one that was too quiet and didn't want to play either. We read about Labrador retrievers, Collies, Poodles, and Airedales.

Next, we decided to go to see the Breeder who lives in the next town. On the way to pick out our perfect puppy, everyone was excited. After checking out all the puppies, we decided to get an airedale puppy. We knew this was the perfect dog for us; he was small and bouncy and looked like he would be a fun addition to our family. We took our puppy home and named him rusty. We are all very happy with the new member of our Family.

1. mom	2. sister
3. pet	4. store
5. collies	6. poodles
7. breeder	8. Airedale
9. Rusty	10. family

© Mark Twain Media, Inc., Publishers 64

Proofreading — Proofreading Review: *Exercise 8*

Name: ______________________ Date: ______________

Proofreading Review: *Exercise 8*

Directions: Proofread the following story, write any colloquialisms in the first column below. In the second column, write the word or phrase in formal English.

I caught a ride with my mom for my first day at Adams Middle School. Since I was the new guy, it was kinda scary because I had to make new friends and meet new teachers. But it went o.k. for the first day, and I figured that I'd catch on in no time.

The next day I was so jittery that my mind went blank. I forgot what my schedule was; I was so embarrassed because I couldn't even find my next class. A teacher saw me wandering in the hall after the bell had rung and helped me find my class. He even gave me a school map. I never did catch his name, but he was one awesome guy!

I am now more than halfway through the school year. My teachers are cool, and I have a group of buddies to hang out with. I can find my classes, no problem. But I will always remember the teacher who helped me at the beginning of the school year.

1. caught a ride	rode
2. new guy	new student
3. kinda	kind of
4. o.k.	okay / all right
5. figured	thought
6. catch on	understand the situation
7. jittery	nervous
8. went blank	forgot everything
9. catch his name	find out his name
10. awesome	terrific
11. cool	excellent / very good
12. buddies	friends
13. hang out	spend time
14. no problem	with no trouble

© Mark Twain Media, Inc., Publishers 65

Proofreading — Proofreading Review: *Exercise 9*

Name: ______________________ Date: ______________

Proofreading Review: *Exercise 9*

Directions: Proofread the following story, using the correct proofreading marks and making changes where necessary.

My favorite season of the year is Summer. I start thinking about it as soon as the snow starts to melt and I feel like the days are getting a little bit warmer. Summer is a time when the swimming are pools open and every one can be out riding ~~its~~ his or her bike or playing tennis. It is hot and humid during the summer where I live, but that is great because you can ~~were~~ wear shorts, sandles, and tank tops, and the sun beats down on you. It is great to soak up the warmth after the cold winter. Summer is the time of year when kids are out of school and have three months to do all the things they have dreamed about doing during the winter. They can do whatever they please. If they want to participate in sports, they can; if they want to sit under a tree in the shade and watch the clouds roll by, they can do that too. Summer is the time you can spend with your friends, but you can also spend time with you family. It's a great time to go on a vacation with your family and visit relatives or a place you have never been before. Summer is the greatest and ~~funnest~~ most fun time.

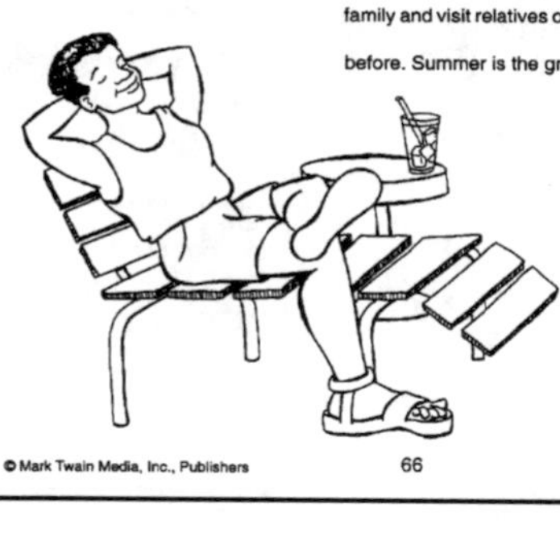

© Mark Twain Media, Inc., Publishers 66

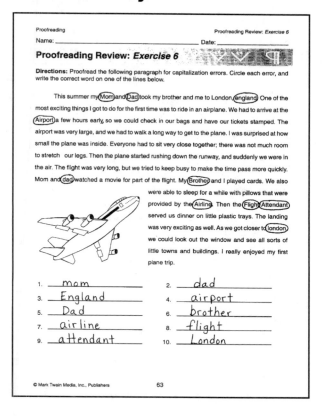

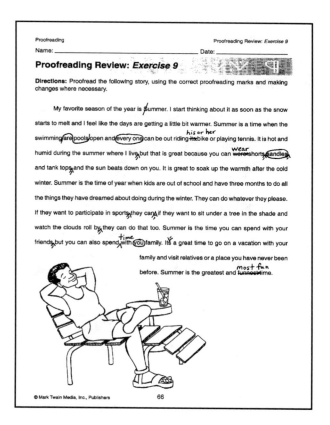

Answer Keys

Name: ______________________ Date: __________

Proofreading Review: *Exercise 10*

Directions: Proofread the following story, using the correct proofreading marks and making changes where necessary.

On our family vacation last year, we traveled to mississippi and visited the gulf coast. It was my first ever trip to the ocean. It was a very long drive to get to the gulf from our house. When we got there we stayed at a hotel that was right on the beach we could walk straight out of our hotel room and be on the sand. We spent nearly every day on the beach. The water was very warm and a beautiful blue green color. My brother and I would spend our time paddeling in the water or building sand castles on the beach. We would also walk up and down the sand after the tide had gone out, looking for shells. We found a hole bunch of different kinds. One day my Mom and Dad rented a sailboat and took us out on to the Gulf we had a great time. A sailboat can go very fast and the boat was rocking so much that my brother got sick! i had the funnest time on our vacation to the beach.

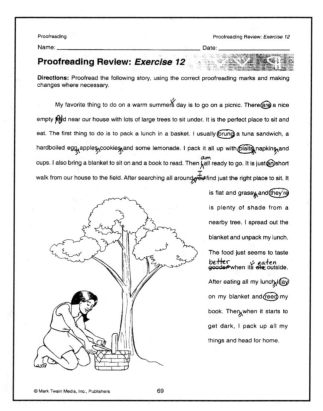

Name: ______________________ Date: __________

Proofreading Review: *Exercise 11*

Directions: Proofread the following story, using the correct proofreading marks and making changes where necessary.

I think that a cat makes the very best sort of pet. We have a cat named Tigger. We gets him from the Humane Society when he was just a kitten. When he was little he was such a cute little cat! He was small with orange fur and a little pink nose. Now that he is more older, he has grown huge. When he was small his favorite trick was to set on a chair and wait for our dog to come by so he could jump on the dogs back. I would yell, Look out! Sometimes that would get the dog to move. Tigger is much older now, so he is not as active. What he really likes to do now is to sit outside in the sun. He is scared of birds, so he like it if someone will sit outside with him. He also likes to eat the grass; really, he likes to eat anything. We feed him dry cat food, but he loves it if he gets a tin of moist food. He gets real excited if someone uses the can opener, even if there is no food for him. Tigger is a silly cat but we love him anyway.

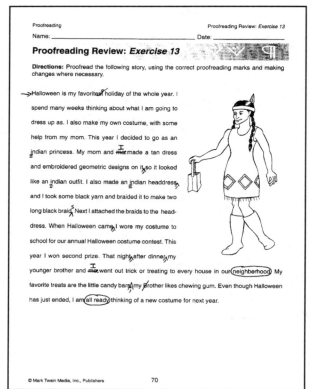

Name: ______________________ Date: __________

Proofreading Review: *Exercise 12*

Directions: Proofread the following story, using the correct proofreading marks and making changes where necessary.

My favorite thing to do on a warm summers day is to go on a picnic. There are a nice empty field near our house with lots of large trees to sit under. It is the perfect place to sit and eat. The first thing to do is to pack a lunch in a basket. I usually brung a tuna sandwich, a hardboiled egg apples cookies and some lemonade. I pack it all up with plaits napkins and cups. I also bring a blanket to sit on and a book to read. Then I all ready to go. It is just an short walk from our house to the field. After searching all around you find just the right place to sit. It is flat and grassy and they're is plenty of shade from a nearby tree. I spread out the blanket and unpack my lunch. The food just seems to taste gooder when its ate outside. After eating all my lunch I lay on my blanket and reed my book. Then when it starts to get dark, I pack up all my things and head for home.

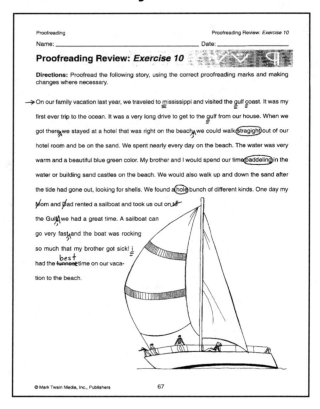

Name: ______________________ Date: __________

Proofreading Review: *Exercise 13*

Directions: Proofread the following story, using the correct proofreading marks and making changes where necessary.

Halloween is my favoritest holiday of the whole year. I spend many weeks thinking about what I am going to dress up as. I also make my own costume, with some help from my mom. This year I decided to go as an indian princess. My mom and me made a tan dress and embroidered geometric designs on it so it looked like an indian outfit. I also made an indian headdress and I took some black yarn and braided it to make two long black braid. Next I attached the braids to the headdress. When Halloween came I wore my costume to school for our annual Halloween costume contest. This year I won second prize. That night after dinner my younger brother and me went out trick or treating to every house in our neighberhood. My favorite treats are the little candy bars my Brother likes chewing gum. Even though Halloween has just ended, I am all ready thinking of a new costume for next year.

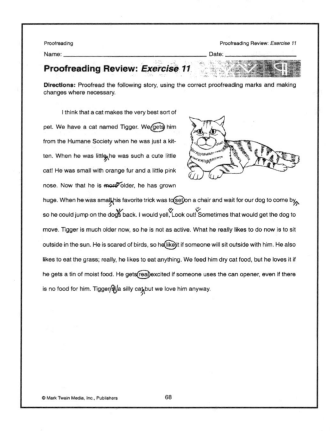

Answer Keys

Proofreading — Proofreading Review: *Exercise 14*

Name: ______________________ Date: ____________

Proofreading Review: *Exercise 14*

Directions: Proofread the following story, using the correct proofreading marks and making changes where necessary.

My Grandfather came over to our house today to help my mother and I bake cookies. We are going to use his special recipie and give them to my Father as a birthday present.

First we went to the grocery stor to buy all the eingredients. We had decided to make chocolate chip cookies because those are his most favoritest ones. We got a grocery cart and filled it up with flour a carton of eggs a bag of sugar chocolate chips and a container of vanilla. We also got my Grandfathers special ingredient: toffee pieces.

After getting home again and unpacking all our ingredients we got out our our mixer and started making the cookies. First we creamed butter and sugar and vanilla, then we added the eggs. When the mixture was smooth and creamy we added flour, salt, and baking soda. Then we stirred in the chocolate chips and the toffee pieces. We had preheated are oven, so we were all set to drop the spoonfuls of cookie dough on the cookie sheet. I like to et the cookie dough even better than the cookies.

When the cookies were done baking and had cooled off we put them in a pretty box decorated with balloons and ties it with a blue ribbon. When we gave it to my Dad, he said, "The cookies are delicious and one of the the best presents I've ever got!

© Mark Twain Media, Inc., Publishers 71

Proofreading — Proofreading Review: *Exercise 15*

Name: ______________________ Date: ____________

Proofreading Review: *Exercise 15*

Directions: Proofread the following story, using the correct proofreading marks and making changes where necessary.

Last year me and my family took a trip to my grandparents house. Since they lived very far a way we decided to take the train. When the day to leave finally came I packed a suitcase and a extra bag with books and a CD player for the trane trip. Wehn we got on the train the first thing we did was pick out our seats. I was able to get one near the window wear I could watch the scenry go by. After a few hours my Brother and I went to the snack car on the train and bought something for dinner. There were all sort of chips candy and hot sandwiches available. I then went over to the observation car this was a part of the train that had had big long windows so passengers could see the countryside. I sat for awhile and watchd farms and small towns go bye. After a few more hours we pulled into the station in my Grandparents town. I think riding the train is an awesome way to travel?

© Mark Twain Media, Inc., Publishers 72

Proofreading — Proofreading Review: *Exercise 16*

Name: ______________________ Date: ____________

Proofreading Review: *Exercise 16*

Directions: Proofread the following story, using the correct proofreading marks and making changes where necessary.

Today I started an after-school job of delivering newspapers for our local newspaper. It is a very cool job because I am earning extra money But it is also a lot of work.

The first thing I do when I get home are to count the number of newspapers that the newspaper office dropped off at my house. I want to make sure that they're are enough to fill all my customers orders. Then I fold each newspaper in half and put it in my large canvas bag. When I am delivering the sunday paper the bag can get very heavy. Since my newspaper route is pretty small I can ride my bike around two deliver the papers. It is important to put everyone paper in the correct spot. Some want it in there mailboxes and others want it put on their front porch. At the end of the month I go around to each customer and collect the newspaper payment and take it down to the newspaper office. I very much enjoy my new after-school job, but its a lot of responsibility.

© Mark Twain Media, Inc., Publishers 73

Proofreading — Proofreading Review: *Exercise 17*

Name: ______________________ Date: ____________

Proofreading Review: *Exercise 17*

Directions: Proofread the following story, using the correct proofreading marks and making changes where necessary.

In the wintertime even though it is cold out and there is lots of snow their are many fun outdoor activites to do. One of my favorite winter activities are skiing. I usually do both downhill and cross coutnry skiing. It is fun to do downhill skiing because of the speed while going down the slopes. With cross-country the speed is slower but it gives you a chance to enjoy the winter scenery.

Sledding si also fun because it doesn't very much equipment and you can do it with a bunch of friends. All that is really needed is a hill and a sled.

The last fun winter activity is ice fishing. Its done by cutting a hole in a frozen lake an catching fish through the ice. It is an activity that requires a lot of patients

© Mark Twain Media, Inc., Publishers 74

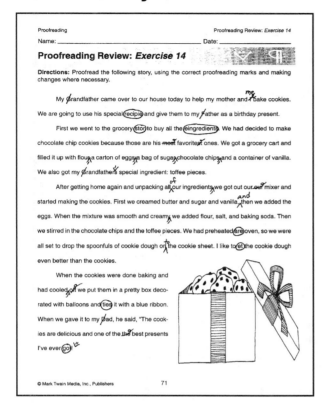

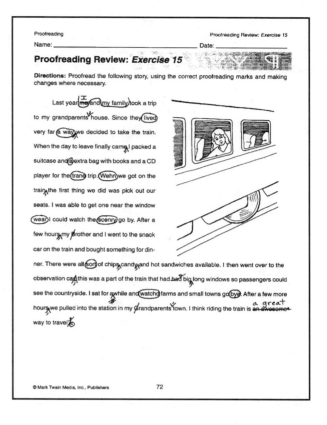

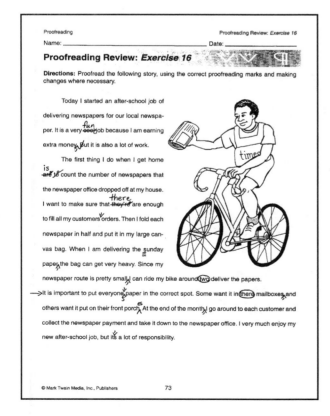

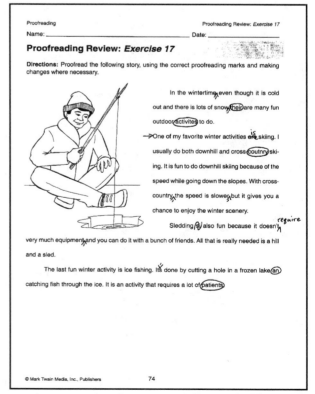

Answer Keys

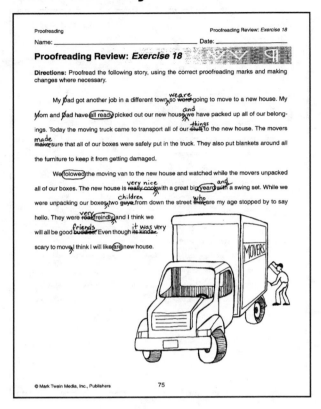

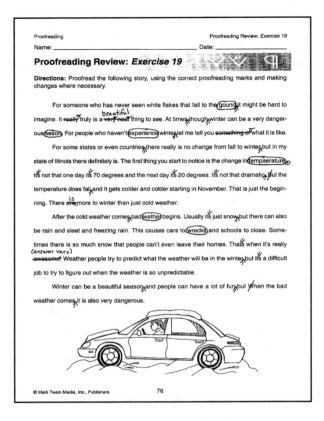

Proofreading Proofreading Review: *Exercise 18*

Name: ______________________ Date: ____________

Proofreading Review: *Exercise 18*

Directions: Proofread the following story, using the correct proofreading marks and making changes where necessary.

My Dad got another job in a different town so were going to move to a new house. My Mom and Dad have all ready picked out our new house we have packed up all of our belongings. Today the moving truck came to transport all of our stuff to the new house. The movers make sure that all of our boxes were safely put in the truck. They also put blankets around all the furniture to keep it from getting damaged.

We folowed the moving van to the new house and watched while the movers unpacked all of our boxes. The new house is really cool with a great big yeard with a swing set. While we were unpacking our boxes two guys from down the street that are my age stopped by to say hello. They were real freindly and I think we will all be good buddies. Even though its kinda scary to move I think I will like are new house.

© Mark Twain Media, Inc., Publishers 75

Proofreading Proofreading Review: *Exercise 19*

Name: ______________________ Date: ____________

Proofreading Review: *Exercise 19*

Directions: Proofread the following story, using the correct proofreading marks and making changes where necessary.

For someone who has never seen white flakes that fall to the gound it might be hard to imagine. It really truly is a very neat thing to see. At times though winter can be a very dangerous seson. For people who haven't experience winter let me tell you something of what it is like.

For some states or even countries there really is no change from fall to winter but in my state of Illinois there definitely is. The first thing you start to notice is the change in tempaerature. Its not that one day its 70 degrees and the next day its 20 degrees. Its not that dramatic but the temperature does fall and it gets colder and colder starting in November. That is just the beginning. There are more to winter than just cold weather.

After the cold weather comes bad wether begins. Usually its just snow but there can also be rain and sleet and freezing rain. This causes cars to wrecks and schools to close. Sometimes there is so much snow that people can't even leave their homes. Thats when it's really awesome. Weather people try to predict what the weather will be in the winter but its a difficult job to try to figure out when the weather is so unpredictable.

Winter can be a beautiful season and people can have a lot of fun but when the bad weather comes it is also very dangerous.

© Mark Twain Media, Inc., Publishers 76

Proofreading Proofreading Review: *Exercise 20*

Name: ______________________ Date: ____________

Proofreading Review: *Exercise 20*

Directions: Proofread the following story, using the correct proofreading marks and making changes where necessary.

Making a sandwich is an easy and fun thing to do. You can fix a sandwich for a snack or for your lunch. Here are you're easy directions.

First you gotta wash your hands with water and soap for about sixty seconds. This is to avoid any contact with germs. Then get out the ingreidients you want to use for you're sandwich. You also need to get out the utensils that youll need to make the sandwich.

To begin take two slices of bread and lightly toast them in the toaster. Wehn the bread are toasted take it out of the toaster and place it on a napkin or plate. Spread mustard or ketchup or mayonaize on each piece of the bred. If you like put a little of each on the toast. Slice a tomato and put one or too slices on one piece of the bread. Take five slices of pickles and put them on top of the tomato. The next thing to put on your bread is the meat. You have a choice of beef, chicken, turkey are salami put one or two slices on your sandwich. Top this off with a slice of cheese either yellow or white cheese is good and sometimes people want both. Add some leafy green lettuce to the sandwich and put your second piece of toast on the sandwich. I hope your mouth is big enough to eat a sandwich like this.

© Mark Twain Media, Inc., Publishers 77

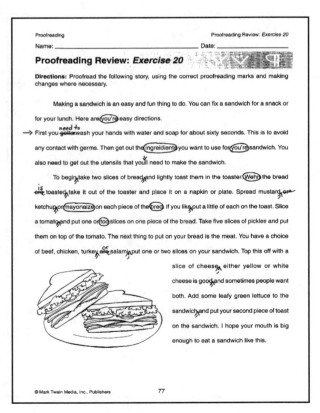